World War II Blitz

Volume 1: 1939-1940

From the Diary of Ruby Thompson

World War II Blitz – Volume 1: 1939-1940

Managing editor - Amanda Meuwissen
Associate editor - Vicki Washuk

Book layout/Cover design - Mario Hernandez

A **BigWorldNetwork.com** Book
Published by BigWorldNetwork.com, LLC
202 North Rock Road | 1303 | Wichita | KS | 67206
www.bigworldnetwork.com

ISBN-13: 978-0615858944
ISBN-10: 0615858945

Second U.S. Edition: August 2013
Printed in the United States of America

FORWARD

Why I chose to publish these Diaries

I am the great-granddaughter of Ruby Alice Side Thompson. I inherited the forty-three diaries that span from 1909–1969. They were given to my grandmother, Ruth Ferris Thompson, wife of Ruby's son, John Thompson. At one time the Diaries were given to my mother, Adele Thompson Aldridge, daughter of Ruth and John Thompson. She keeps a journal herself and tells me she is now on #100.

I recently started re-reading the diaries written during World War II and found them most interesting and worthy of being seen by others. I realized how little I knew about the events surrounding World War II and what Londoners in particular had to endure. These diaries are personal experiences and opinions of Ruby's marriage and the war she lived through, often not knowing if her house would be the next target of destruction.

I cannot imagine having to endure these experiences. Ruby was not able to express her opinions or feelings about either the war or her marriage except in the privacy of her Diary. When her sons read these diaries after their mother's death in 1970, it has been reported that they were shocked about her relationship with their father. Apparently Ruby was an expert at keeping much of her feelings to herself while she was starkly open about them when writing in her journal.

I thought that others might also find these diaries of interest and started posting a blog for the World War II Diary. In doing so I received reactions from people from around the world and this inspired me to publish them in book form for all to enjoy.

These are Ruby's outpourings of her experience during the Blitz bombings that she could not always speak about. Many of the things she says would be considered politically incorrect in today's world. Some of her opinions will be disturbing to some people. To edit out Ruby's opinions would be a disservice to Ruby so her words will stand as she wrote them.

This is volume one of a four volume series of the diaries written between 1939 and 1945.

Victoria Aldridge Washuk

World War II Blitz

Volume 1: 1939-1940

From the Diary of Ruby Thompson

Parental Guidance, some themes may be unsuitable for younger readers.

BigWorldNetwork.com
Kansas

WHO'S WHO IN RUBY'S DIARY

Ruby Alice Side — Writer of the diary and oldest child of Eliza and Charles Side. Born April 18, 1884 at Fulham; London, England. Baptized at St. Stephen's Church, Shepherds Bush. Married Edward (Ted) Thompson at St. John's Protestant Episcopalian Church, May 2, 1905 in Bayonne, New Jersey, USA. Died January 17, 1970.

Edward (Ted) Thompson — (Ruby's husband) Born July 17, 1879. Died March 24, 1970.

Eliza Alice Searle Side — Mother of Ruby Alice. 2nd child of John Searle and Mary Ann Beates, born at Nottinghill, England, February 10, 1863. Died November 29, 1942. Married Charles Henry Side (father of Ruby); born June 7, 1859; died August 8, 1928.

Herbert Thompson — Eldest brother of Ted, born October 4, 1868; died 1948.

Selma Thompson — Daughter of Herbert Thompson.

Bertie Thompson — Son of Herbert Thompson.

RUBY AND TED THOMPSON HAD SEVEN SONS:

Edward Augustine Thompson (Eddie) — born 1906; died 1968.

Harold Francis Thompson — born 1908; died unknown date.

John Henry Thompson (Father of Adele Thompson Aldridge and grandfather to Vicki Aldridge Washuk) — born 1910; died 2002.

Stephen Gerard Thompson (Jimmie) — born 1912; died 1973.

Charles Hilary Thompson (Charlie) — born 1914; died unknown date.

Alfred Cuthbert Thompson (Cuthie / Sket) — born 1919; died unknown date; was in the R.A.F. and taken as prisoner of war. After the war, married Rita Pullan.

Arthur Frederick Thompson (Artie) — Twin to Cuthie; born 1919; died 1991.

TABLE OF CONTENTS

EPISODE #1

- *FRIDAY, SEPTEMBER 1, 1939* -

War started today. After another week of lies and duplicity, Hitler launched into actual warfare early this morning. At five thirty this morning he announced the enclosure of Danzig in the Reich, and at five forty-five he bombed his first Polish town. Reports were that the Germans had already bombed eight Polish cities, and were attacking on all frontiers.

The BBC has just announced that King George held a Privy Council this noon, and has signed papers completing the mobilization of our Army, Navy, and Air Forces. Further news is to be broadcast at four p.m.

- *SUNDAY, SEPTEMBER 3, 1939* -

At eleven fifteen today Mr. Chamberlain broadcast from number Ten Downing Street. He said: This morning the British Ambassador in Berlin handed the German government a final note stating that, unless we heard from them by eleven o'clock, that they were prepared at once to withdraw their troops from Poland, a state of war would exist between us.

I have to tell you that no such undertaking has been received, and that consequently this country is at war with Germany. He ended his speech like this: "Now may God bless you all. May he defend the right. It is the evil things that we shall be fighting against, brute force, bad faith, injustice, oppression and persecution, and against them I am certain that the right will prevail."

He had scarcely finished speaking when the air raid signals sounded. Naturally we all took cover. About twelve o'clock the all-clear signal came. We thought it had been the Germans, of course, but in tonight's news we were told, that it was a strange aircraft, which had been sighted over the Channel, and that when it had been identified, it was found to be a friendly plane, and allowed to pass. However, the warnings were a shock. It was such a beautiful day, sunny and with clear skies. At five o'clock the French government broadcast a similar statement to Mr. Chamberlain, saying they had no reply from Hitler and that as of five o'clock the French were at war with Germany.

So here is the war. We have been fending it off for years, but at last it is here. The folly of men is now going to destroy men. Force will fight force. Maybe the right will prevail. I don't know. I can only hope so. God keep us all!

- MONDAY, SEPTEMBER 4, 1939 -

In the middle of the night we were wakened from sleep by the air raid sirens. We got up, closed all the windows, put on our robes and went downstairs. Here we remained in the passage by the staircase until the all-clear signal came, about four o'clock. The kitchen clock struck three whilst I was waking Artie. However, we were informed at nine this morning that this was again caused by the passage of unidentified aircraft over Essex and the midland counties; our fighters went up, identified the airplane and then returned to ground. We are not told exactly what planes they were or why they were flying over England at three in the morning.

Real news of war came early. The Atlantic Liner, *Athena*, was torpedoed off the west of the Hebrides, and sank at five o'clock this morning. She had fourteen hundred people aboard, most of them Americans returning home. She was from Glasgow, bound for Montreal. Now, noon, we are informed that a notice has been posted in Glasgow, signed, Cook, Master, stating that all passengers and crew, except those killed by the explosion, were got safely into the boats, and many of them had already been picked up by other vessels. President Roosevelt broadcast in the States last night that America would stay neutral. However, if the Germans attack the Americans on the seas, what then?

It is eight thirty p.m. and I am in a blaze of anger. At seven o'clock Ted said, "I'm going down to Forest Gate, to see what traveling is like in the dark." He went too! Now, all lights are forbidden, all cinemas closed, all gatherings, indoor, and outside, prohibited, because of the danger from bombs. No lights in the trains or the busses, no lights in automobiles. Ted has to go to Forest Gate to see his precious guild of course, his pious and adoring spinsters and oafs. Well, it may be fine Catholic piety, but its damned bad husbandry. All around many women are ill and hysterical, and very bad when the air raid signals sound. It is nerves and they can't help it.

What does Ted care about me? It is night, the raiding signals may be heard at any moment but I am left alone in the house, to endure it as best I can. The Catholic Evidence Guild is of very great importance to Ted, but I am of no importance at all. This heartlessness at a time like this fills me with dismay. I cannot believe he would act so, yet he does. He goes off on his own pleasuring, danger or no danger, and I am left alone, danger or no danger. Anyhow I am in a fretful mood, and have been, all this time of gathering tension. I think of Cuthie, who is surely going to immediate death and of Artie who will follow him. I think of my boys in America, who I cannot reach and their children whom I have never seen. In my heart I am crying and crying.

The lot my husband has imposed upon me is a cruel one. He has denuded me of my children, and of himself as lover and friend. Now he leaves me to face terror alone, as well as desolation. I know there may be no raid before he returns but the chances are equal there may be. I say he has no right to leave me alone at such a time. It is a cruel thing to do. It hurts me, and it angers me, and I feel I shall never forgive him. But I suppose I shall! What is there else to do? I have to excuse him. I say he is crazy. I am angry just the same, very angry. He has no business to treat me like this, with such callousness. Loving kindness, he just doesn't know what it is: ordinary friendliness, he doesn't know that either. As Eddie says, "He's not human."

- *SUNDAY, SEPTEMBER 10, 1939* -

The war has now completed one week. All week the weather has been perfect. All summer it has been very poor, no warmth, nor sun, nor brightness at all. Now it has cleared up and we have had more sun and warmth and clearness in this past week than in all the rest of the summer put together. A good thing too for it has kept people's spirits up. It is hard to be melancholy in perfect weather.

The Germans, of course, are overrunning Poland, that was to be expected. There are reports they have taken

Warsaw and counter-reports that they haven't, but it is not known yet for a fact.

Old Bert has closed Arden Cottage and gone to live in Ongar. So have Bertie and Peggy. Bertie comes into business every day, but not old Bert. He is scared stiff. Ted behaves as usual, and he goes to mass every morning. Ted is the complete escapist.

Ted is more talkative than ever. I listen and listen, and I just despise him as a silly fool. Also he is more critical. He has been criticizing Artie to me for a long time but now he has begun picking on the boy directly. Artie answers back. They had a spat together in the scullery this morning about a pane of picture glass, which after hanging about the garden for months, had been smashed and Artie had cleared away the fragments. Today Ted missed that piece of glass, and gave Artie one of his typical cross-examinations about it. The boy answered politely but Ted then began to read him a lecture about carelessness, about laziness, about impoliteness, about being brusque, and so on.

Artie got riled. He said, "I resent those remarks. They are not true." Ted went on some more. Artie said, "I still resent your remarks. You know that I am the only one who makes any attempt to clear up the place here and to keep it neat. I didn't know you wanted the glass. It had stood around for weeks and weeks and you never mentioned it. It got broken. I cleared up the pieces. Why should I have to tell you? I think your remarks are uncalled for and unkind."

The word "unkind" got under Ted's skin. He answered sarcastically "Thank You" and walked away into the parlor. Ted fancy's an idea of himself as a benefactor. It's all a part of his general interfering "doing well" he calls it. I've endured it for years, over and over again. The reprobates he dreams he is reforming have cheated me.

Sucker after sucker has found out Ted for a good thing. He's never cared. He always thinks the next "deserving case" will answer to his interest and charity with reform and with gratitude. So to tell him he is unkind is too much for him.

He is unkind. He has a most malicious tongue which he exercises on all those who can't or don't round on him. Now it's got to Artie's turn. Cuthie has got away. He made Cuthie miserable with his nagging for years all for Cuthie's 'good' of course! We said, "Hell!" Now it's Artie that's wrong. Artie, apparently, is going to answer back.

Oh, Ted and his moralizing, his sarcasms, his belittling, his sneers, oh, what a disagreeable person he is to live with! Yet he never suspects it! He thinks and says that he is broad minded, just, kind, and courteous. Whereas actually, he is fanatically narrow-minded, spiteful, mean, secretive, intolerant, and intolerable.

This week he has been awful. I say as little as possible. Silence is the only way to protect oneself from him but he makes me feel that I regard him either as an utter fool, or as a very hateful man. I don't want to feel or think like that about him. I don't want him to upset me. I want to keep serene. I want to keep myself. I want to keep free from him, untouched by his follies, unconfined by his limitations, impervious by his lack of love, not biased against the truth because of his peculiar prejudices that is it. I want to be free of him, inviolate.

EPISODE #2

- MONDAY, SEPTEMBER 11, 1939 -

Miss Jude arrived at ten fifteen this morning and stayed until four thirty. She was here two days last week also. She exhausts me. She talks in her noisy Irish way without ceasing. Such rubbish! Today she went on and on about the Archangel Michael, and how he will protect the Poles. Also about Teresa Neumann and what she will be "seeing" about the war. About Saint Peter, about Saint John Bosco, the late Pope, and a man in Brazil who has visions and prophesies. She undid her blouse and unfastened a bunch of medals from her corset to show me. She expounded about the Green Scapular, and how it can be hung on a picture. In effect, she dazed me.

I think she is the most credulous and the most superstitious woman I have ever known. Worse than any of the Polish and Austrian girls who used to pass through my kitchen. They, at least, were peasants, many of them unable to read or write, but Mrs. Jude is supposed to be an educated woman. She positively wears me out with her ceaseless rubbishy chatter. When she left, she forgot her bag, so Mary Bernadette came this evening to fetch it.

Mary, who returned to her job this week, was telling us something of how things look in the city. Ted, of course, did not go to Forest Gate tonight. The Guild has had to close down. All street meetings, processions, crowds, etc. are forbidden. Anyhow, even if they weren't, you couldn't hold a meeting anywhere in the pitch-dark streets. However, this is not any sort of ending or a suspension of the Guild, which makes any difference to me. I asked Ted to give up the Guild for my sake; he refused. Now he hasn't given up the Guild, the Guild has given up him automatically, because it ceases to function. So I still don't go to mass. I think I am more Un-Catholic than ever. I have NO belief in the Roman Church and I don't want to have. It has, I think, quite ceased to matter to me. Well, here in the Guild is another example of Ted's childish obstinacy. He just wouldn't give up the Guild because it was a matter of vital importance to me. He just refused to give it up, like the matter of moving the bed. It's a sort of moron obstinacy, which he shares, with Selma.

So tonight he has been sitting in the parlor and reading a book entitled, *The Interior Life.* There are four hundred pages of it, close dissection of the movements of the soul, translated from the French. Naturally, no Englishman could ever write this sort of stuff. This is the sort of treatise which makes religion a dramatically difficult intellectual exercise, which takes it away from the simple, and makes it esoteric; it is a caustic argument, by the elect, for the elect. Well, religion is not an argument, and to my thinking, and to my experience, this sort of book is a damnable obstacle in the way of any vital flowing real religion. It is the product of a sheltered theologian, and has nothing whatever to do with live religion. Ted sits and reads it, four hundred pages of words. The Interior Life! What Ted needs is something about the exterior life, something about blood and the natural affections, not precise statements of logical arguments. Oh well, I suppose nothing will ever alter Ted, not even another war, right here on our doorstep. Theology is a boon to Ted. He can talk about it forever.

Yesterday the Russians invaded Poland on the East. This is the end of Poland. What is it the beginning?

I hoped for letters from America this morning, but there were none. Anyhow, I had made up my mind to cable the boys, so I dressed and was out by half past nine. I went directly to the post office and cabled Harold and Jim care of the Herald Tribune. I asked them to combine, and get me into America. I asked them to see the immigration officials, and send me a permit and passage, or cash, quickly. I intend to do everything I can to get away. Ted answered an inquiry that he would rather be in England with a war on, than in America with peace forever. Well, I wouldn't. England is weariness to me at any time, and in wartime it would be hell. The twins are among the doomed. Airmen, God keep them! I don't want to be here when they come home on leave. I don't want to be here when they are wounded or killed. I don't want to be here, shut up with Ted and his pettiness and paltriness. I want to get where my "safe" children are, with their little ones. I want the happiness of being with my children for a little while before I die. I want to be in America, the land that I love.

Maybe I won't be able to do it, maybe the boys won't help, maybe the consul won't give me a visa, and maybe Ted will obstruct me. I don't know.

I am going to try to get to America, with all my might, and once there I will never return here again. I am sick of England, and the whole fantastic life Ted makes me live.

From the post office I went into the arcade and into Jean Claire's, the tailor. I ordered a warm woolen coat, paid a deposit on it, and am to go for a fitting on Saturday. Then I went into Stone's and bought a supply of buttons and sewing silks, and now I am going to get set to sewing. I have some nylon to make nightgowns, and some black cloth to make a dress. I intend to work systematically on getting my wardrobe in order for traveling. So, Au-Revoir.

- *WEDNESDAY, SEPTEMBER 20, 1939* -

I want to pin down a dream before it evaporates. For a long time I have noticed that my dreams are practically all of the past, especially my life in Bayonne, when I was young and having babies. Sometimes they are of the even remoter past, and it was such a dream I had last night. I was dreaming of Sydenham Whitelock. I was reliving that moment when he and I stood together on Barnes Old Bridge, isolated there one sunny Sunday afternoon, and had an intense vibrant awareness of each other, and the world around us, and ourselves, electric to one another, pausing in a moment of communication, understanding, love, and bliss. My God! That was nearly forty years ago!

Then we were together in Grandma's house, standing in the hall, outside her parlor door, aware of her and her vitality, in there, in her room, and we merged in a wordless embrace. I felt his kisses, I heard his heart beating, and every nerve in me was responding in delight to his strength and virility, his vitality and health, his manliness, and personal affection. I knew that Syd Whitelock loved me not as a woman but as Ruby myself.

Into the ecstasy of this dreaming broke the noise of the movements of Ted getting up. My wakening mind flashed recognition of this silly insignificant fool who is my husband. He dropped on his knees to pray, presently the door banged, and he had gone out to church. I despised him with an abysmal despising. This fool, who wasted his life in daydreaming and sacrifices reality to the unending pursuit of a medieval sacrament!

Yes, I can read my dream in the Freudian explanations. It is the expostulation of my body protesting against its sexual deprivations. My life with Ted is one long mental and physical frustration. I am an ardent and passionate being and I had the misfortune to marry a milksop, and stupidly I didn't remedy the error before it was too late. If I had any sense of all about us, I would have divorced Ted twenty years ago. However, I didn't. Now I am an old woman, and a divorce would be no advantage to me. So, when I sleep, when the Censor sleeps, my inner secret woman compensates herself with a phantasm. Awake, I know it is a phantasm and a trick. Thank God I never lose my sense of realities. Ted has a faculty of fooling himself, but I haven't that faculty. Ted says I am a materialist. This is a condemnation, and is contra distinction to an idealist, which he considers himself to be, and something very good. To me "idealist" signifies fool, more often than not, and a very obstinate unreasonable fool to boot. I would describe myself as a realist. I have lived as a realist for a very long time, and I expect to die as such.

- *THURSDAY, SEPTEMBER 21, 1939* -

I had a visit from Miss Canham this morning, in quick answer to the letter I sent her yesterday. I find I am too nervous to sew, so I wrote and asked her could she do some work for me immediately.

She will, so good luck. She carried away the piece of black cloth, to make into a modish afternoon dress; also two old garments to make over into "new" ones, and my black figured silk dress which I haven't worn all this year, to be altered slightly and brought up to date.

I have been lying awake thinking about my clothes, and here are my ideas, which she will execute. First: She will work on my blue figured panne velvet gown, which I had new to take to America in 1933. It has been out of date for several years, but the velvet is as good as ever. So I thought it would make over into a peplum blouse, with soft sheered swatches to form the shoulder, to cross the bosom surplice style, and fasten at the back. She has taken that. Also, second, to wear with it my loose three-quarter raglan coat, of very fine black wool, which I made to wear to the movies on summer nights; I thought this would make over into a full gored evening skirt. She says it will, and she has taken that.

She will come next Tuesday for fittings. Then I had thoughts about my old winter coat. Since I have ordered a new one as I have, the old one should make over into a smart tailored frock; and Miss Canham says she can make it into such. Out of the lining, which is very good quality crepe-de-chine, she can make me a petticoat. So I shall have a few presentable and fashionable garments, for traveling or whatever occasion I have to meet. My underwear I will attend to myself. I have nearly finished one nightgown, and have enough nylon on hand to make another. Meanwhile, before Tuesday, I am going to partially unpick my black coat, take off the fur, etc. So work is proceeding in anticipation of getting away. Of course there is no certainty I can get away, but I am going to be ready to go.

- *FRIDAY, SEPTEMBER 22, 1939* -

Once, some years ago, when Auntie Lizzie was staying here, a very lovely thing happened to me. I was sitting one morning by the sink, peeling vegetables, when Auntie walked through into the scullery; and she came up behind my chair and without a word, she stooped and kissed the back of my neck. That was a spontaneous act of affection, and I have never forgotten it. It was a lovely gesture from a very old woman. I was remembering it this morning when I wakened. Those are the sorts of gestures, which make life beautiful, the signs of affection, which I crave.

Ted was remarking rather recently that someone in America once told him he was cold blooded, and he couldn't believe it. Yet that is exactly what he is though apparently he doesn't think so. My instinct when I woke this morning was to turn to Ted and take him in my arms. I didn't because the gesture would have been useless. He would have only repulsed me. He couldn't turn to me. He only turns to the church. I think, just as it is natural for the flower to turn towards sun, the baby to its mother, the dog to its master, friend-to-friend, lover-to-lover, so it is natural for husband and wife to turn towards each other. However, it is not natural with Ted.

I remember many years ago, whilst we still lived in Mrs. McKnight's house, and Ted was sleeping in the little room. I went into him in that room one night, and he took me by the shoulders and put me out and shut the door. Those sorts of actions bruise the heart. It has always been useless for me to ask for love, or to make any offer of love, so far as Ted is concerned. When his lust drives him, then I must take him no matter what my inclination or disinclination.

Well, I don't consider that love. To me, the first essential of love is friendliness and Ted has no friendliness. That hour of brotherly sweetness, hand in hand, Ted has no conception of and never had. That is what I want, and have always wanted.

It seems to me that in a good marriage, a couple could lay embraced without any prick of lust, could fall asleep on an encircling arm, could wake to smile, to touch in friendliness, and to speak in tender friendliness. It is not to be with Ted. His ideal is the bloodless and gutless saint, and he rises without word or touch, and goes to his everlasting church. No, I should have no compunctions about leaving him. He doesn't need me, doesn't want me, doesn't love me, and doesn't want my love. This is the sad truth.

EPISODE #3

- TUESDAY, SEPTEMBER 26, 1939 -

A letter from Harold arrived this morning by airmail. He tells me he and Charlie are seeing the immigration officials, and will both fill out the necessary forms and affidavits, and forward them to me by the next mail. He tells me once over there I will need no money, and I can live in Baldwin with him forever. What a relief!

After supper I showed the letter to Ted. He was surprised, but asked me, was it right that I would prefer to live with the boys, and did I really want to go to America? I said, yes, please. He said, all right, and he wouldn't put any obstacles in my way. He also added that certainly he would pay my passage, and would see if he could make me an allowance. This, I think, because he was piqued by Harold's remarks about money. Anyhow, he did make the offer.

- FRIDAY, SEPTEMBER 29, 1939 -

The neighborhood women considerably plague me. They keep coming here all the time—Mrs. Jude, Mrs. James, Mrs. Archer, Mrs. Lee, Mrs. Stanford—if it isn't one it's the other, and I can't get a minute to myself. They say I'm so placid. If they only knew!

It is St. Francis of Assisi. Also, it is old Bert's birthday. He is seventy-one today. Tomorrow he returns to Arden Cottage, having had enough of Ongar. Ted is telling tales of him with love and admiration. In my opinion, Herbert is a selfish, uncouth, uncultured, cowardly old fool. He is nearly as brainless as Selma, and quite as obstinate. He made his money through shrewdness, cunning, and luck. Ted mistakes him as one of the examples of the fortunate ones who were never cramped in their moneymaking careers by too much education.

Ted said to me, "I think you have suffered through your ability to read and write. If you hadn't learned how to read, think how much trouble and unhappiness you would have saved yourself, how much better off you would have been! Look at some of the old-timers around here; there are some of the richest who can't even sign their own names, but that didn't prevent them making money, did it? Why, education would have been a downright disadvantage to them!"

I said, "I think it is a horrible thing to say."

"Education isn't everything," he fenced. Of course it isn't; but to say that people are lucky because they didn't get any is a perfectly abominable statement to make.

I said no more, but I was disgusted. Like one day recently when Ted put up a boost for hypocrisy. We had been talking about Hitler and his absurd speeches, and about cynicism. "Well," said Ted, "after all, there is a good deal to be said in favor of the Victorian hypocrisy. The hypocrite at least believed in a standard virtue, and in truth and purity and honor: he knew he was against the right and tried to hide his wrongness; but these fellows today, what do they care about goodness? They don't even pretend to hide their vices. They don't admit the codes even! The hypocrite at least tried not to shock the world. Yes, there's something to be said for hypocrisy, and I'd rather encounter a good hypocrite any day than one of these modern don't-care-you-go-to-hell fellows!"

Well, I wouldn't. I made no reply to this. What was there to say? It simply struck me so 'Catholic', an apology for secretiveness and dishonesty; here is the Catholic who doesn't demand real goodness but only the appearance of goodness. My God! It makes me sick.

SATURDAY, OCTOBER 7, 1939

Stone's man came this morning bringing the dark window blinds I ordered on September 4th for the black out. Ted opened the door to him, and then called out to me, "Hi, Lady! Did you order these shades for the last war, or this one?" Already we are feeling the pinch in many commodities. Stone's say they cannot fill their orders for blinds, because they cannot get the materials.

I have been to town, to the warehouse, to buy sheets and pillowcases, and they haven't gotten any. There has been a scarcity of sugar for weeks. Last week I couldn't buy tea. This week I couldn't buy lard. Soon now we shall have ration cards, but it doesn't follow we shall be able to get rations.

SUNDAY, OCTOBER 8, 1939

There is news from Zurich today of the beating up of Frau Anna Zeigler, the Nazi's Women's Leader. She was speaking somewhere in the Ruhr district, and told the women Hitler was very angry with them, because they were not keeping up the morale of their men, and that he would treat them like soldiers. This made her audience so angry, so wild, that they stormed the platform and beat her up and scratched her so severely that she had to be taken to the hospital. The Gestapo police arrested nineteen women. The women shouted that they had no husbands, and they had no food. I should think they would be wild. If a man gave them such a line of talk they would just consider him some fool of a man, let him talk himself out, and pay no attention. For a woman to talk to them in this fashion is treason to the sex and I should think they would beat her up.

I am surprised at what we do hear about the submission of the German women. We were told one day that when the women would be waiting in the food queues to get their family rations, and sometimes having to wait for hours, Army Louie's would drive up, impress a load of women, take them to the barracks, and make them cook and scrub for the soldiers. The excuse given was that since they had plenty of time to wait in the lines, they had plenty of time for other purposes, so they must work for their country, and do whatever the Government told them. This sort of thing is outrageous but why do the women submit to it? The soldiers, by brute force, could compel the women to go to the barracks, but they couldn't compel them to peel vegetables, or to scrub; and surely even the Germans wouldn't be such fiends as to kill them for refusing. I can't imagine Englishwomen submitting to such masculine tyranny. If our Tommie's gathered up a load of women from Romford market, I think they'd find they'd got a load of wildcats to deal with.

MONDAY, OCTOBER 9, 1939

Can a leopard change its spots? I don't think so. Ted was born and brought up in a mushy mawkish Evangelical atmosphere. His parents were Methodist Salvationist fundamentalists, and very ignorant people. His father was a drunk, alternating soaks with repentance. They went to Chapel and they had family prayers in the parlor every night, when everyone in turn had to pray aloud extempore. It must have been awful for violence and crudity of emotion and belief, and for lack of knowledge and dignity. Ted absorbed it all, and has never gotten over it. He can't disbelieve the lurid Christian story. That's why Catholicism fits him so easily, and that's why he is not revolted by the materialism of the Catholic religion, for it is only an extension, and another facet, of the sort of religion he was bred to.

As for me, I never was a Christian. I've spent thirty years trying to believe the Christian religion, trying to hammer it into me or me into it and I can't accept it. I think I must have been born a skeptic. As for my father, he was a skeptic. Born in a good middle class family, educated at Charterhouse, he became the gentlemanly conservative agnostic and skeptic of the brilliant nineties. My father had an exploring mind, and an appreciating one. Brought up in the Church of England, he was intrigued by the High Church movement in his youth, but by the time I could remember him, he had stopped going to church, and had, instead, become interested in The Theistic Church, and Charles Voysey.

He became tired of that, too, and had ceased going there before I became a regular attendant about 1899 or 1900. When I became interested in Theosophy, my father came with me to Theosophical lectures in Albemarle Street; and later when 'Higher Thought' gained my interest, he used to come with me to The Higher Thought Center in Kensington High Street. When I think of Dad now, I realize that he never condemned any kind of thought, or any kind of thinker. He was interested in all thought. That's why he was interested in all the arts, as well as all the philosophies, and that's why he couldn't endure a fool.

So with me, I think Ted such a fool, and he bores me so desperately I don't know how to endure him. I listen to his fool talk; talk about politics, about America, about religion, about art (of which he knows nothing!) and he sounds sillier and sillier. Ted has always been talkative, but now he is becoming downright garrulous. I listen to him because I can't help myself, but inside, my secret woman is exclaiming, you silly old fool! You bloody silly fool! So these past few weeks I have been turning back to some of the old books, which at different times sustained me.

When I have to live in this world that men have made, especially this Europe, run by male maniacs, I feel most vehemently that I have no use for men, and I will not agree with them about any of their affairs. Why should I pay attention to what men say? That's why I am feeling so absolutely anti-Christian, swinging back to what I was in my beginnings, anti-Christian. What can a man tell me about God? What's a priest, but a man? I have produced men, brought them to birth, suckled them, brought them to maturity, through every indignity of the flesh, and no man can tell me anything, unless it is the rare man like Emerson or Whitman, who are talking about spirit and principles, not about other men.

That's why my mind turns to Mary Baker Eddy. I know she did not live an impeccable life. I know her literary style was atrocious; but in spite of all her ignorance's and defects, she was saying something that set women free of men. An American woman, with an American religion, and I can understand and appreciate both. In the same way Adela Curtis was saying and doing the same thing for English women, only she wasn't clever enough to get into the limelight. The same things with Mary Austin, trying to work free in art and plot maps of genius, religion, and psychology. Mary Cady Stanton, trying to free women submitted to men's dictums. They felt they were themselves, in their own woman pattern, and so will I.

No man can speak for me, or think for me, no matter how renowned he is in goodness and cleverness. I will think for myself and speak for myself as much as I dare. I have even been reading old Harriet Martineau. It's one hundred years since she asserted herself as an independent being. I want my Mary Beard. I loaned her book, *Concerning Women,* to Dorrie Stanforth more than a year ago, and she hasn't returned it yet. I suspect she can't read it.

That's why I want to go to America, the country where people are not narrow-minded in traditions and religions of the past, and where women are accorded equality with men.

EPISODE #4

- THURSDAY, OCTOBER 12, 1939 -

It is Columbus Day in America. Very appropriately my 'papers' arrived from America today. I now have all the necessary affidavits, from Harold and from Charlie, with which to approach the American Consul and ask for a visa. I have not mentioned them to Ted, as there did not seem to offer a propitious moment.

A very dear letter from Charlie was enclosed. He said that for eight years it has been his ambition to offer me a home in America. What I did today was to write to the United States Lines Office in the Haymarket, and ask for a sailing list.

- FRIDAY, OCTOBER 13, 1939 -

It is Arthur Thompson's birthday. Had he lived I think he would have been 53 today. Had he lived, I wonder if he would have grown as peculiar as his brothers?

Continuing my preliminaries, this morning I telephoned Dr. Mauro and asked her whether she would give me duplicate statements to the effect that I was an honest and respectable person, etc. She agreed immediately, and told me she would leave them for me in her office at midday, which she did, and for which I am truly grateful. Last year I asked Father Bishop for these. He agreed to give them to me, after Mr. Thompson had been informed. This was quite all right with me then. Now, this year, I am quite certain I don't want any Catholic to stand as sponsor for me. I will re-enter the states as I first went in: as a Protestant Englishwoman, and a member of the Church of England. (Confirmed in the Protestant Episcopal Church of America.) If I am really able to separate my life from Ted's life, I will certainly separate myself in total from Ted's church.

Then, this afternoon, I went round to Victoria Road and had some fresh passport photos taken at Madeline Myles.

Tonight I asked Ted for some money to pay for my coat, which will be ready tomorrow. I have still not told him of the arrival of my affidavits. I think he thinks I have abandoned the idea of going to America! I don't know when I will tell him. When I collect my passport photos I shall then have all the items the Consul demands before they will consider the request for an Immigration visa. Charlie writes me that he has sent in an official request to Washington asking for a special preference permit for me, and that Bill Berry and Ruth Eason witnessed for him on the affidavit he had to send there.

- SATURDAY, OCTOBER 14, 1939 -

There is news today of the sinking of the Royal Oak. Her compliment of men was approximately 1200; so far, only 370 are known to be survivors. This is worse than the loss of the Courageous. On Thursday of this week Mr. Chamberlain, speaking in Parliament, scorned Hitler's so-called peace offer of last week. Since Thursday the war has intensified. So it will go on, of course. Probably on the Western front it has not yet really begun. We are told that we have transported to France one hundred and fifty-eight thousand men and twenty-five thousand vehicles without a single casualty. This week's news is most seriously concerned with Finland. Russia has already swallowed Latvia and Estonia, and sent messages to Finland that she wished to negotiate concerning airbases and airports in Finland. Finland's answer was to mobilize. Finland insists on being free Finland. Every day the news gets worse and worse, madder and madder. Europe is the place to get away from.

- *MONDAY, OCTOBER 16, 1939* -

This morning Artie received notification that he must report for the Army Militia, at Victoria, on Wednesday the 18th.

- *TUESDAY, OCTOBER 17, 1939* -

Artie cleared up at the office yesterday morning and has been clearing up around the house ever since. He has been to see the R.A.F. Officer, because he was passed and accepted for a pilot, but he is told he must report to the militia as called; perhaps a transfer can be arranged. He has not been called for the air before this, because they have been taking men who have been serving in the Civil Air Guard. He was shown his name as tenth on the list to be called, and was given a letter to this effect, to be given to the receiving officer tomorrow, at Victoria. It does seem silly to put him in the Militia, when they know he is "passed" for the air.

- WEDNESDAY, OCTOBER 18, 1939 -

Artie left with Ted this morning. Tonight he phoned us that he is in the London Scottish Branch of the Gordon Highlanders and can be addressed: Company D. 59 Buckingham Gate. I was so miserable and restless after he went that I went to town myself, leaving Mrs. Shaw to carry on in the house, and get Ted's dinner and tea for him.

I went straight to Hammersmith. Found Polly sitting by the fire, looking gloomy as hell, so took mother out forthwith. Took her over to the co-op to buy a pair of black slippers, and there in the shop told her of my plans and prospects for going to America. Naturally she was surprised, but just as naturally she was more interested in my immediate purchases than in my immediate news. I bought three hats (a russet velvet beret, a rose velvet turban, and a black felt tricorne). I also bought three scarves to go with them, and four pairs of gloves, besides the black slippers. Silly purchases, but I had to do something! Then we went back to the house, and Mother made some sandwiches for me, and we had tea. I left soon after four o'clock. I decided on my way over I wasn't going to travel through London in the dark. London is now so ghastly awful, already a city of the dead.

- SATURDAY, OCTOBER 21, 1939 -

I was surprised at teatime by Cuth and Artie walking in together. I was expecting Cuth for a weekend visit, but not Artie. They had met at Liverpool Street and traveled out together. Artie was in what is known as "Battle Dress," including a huge khaki overcoat and a tin hat. All the fellows had been sent home, and to stay the night, mainly, it would seem, so that they might bring home their entire private clothes and belongings. All the same, as I go about my preparations I begin to feel sad. I will not let this sadness conquer my resolution to go. Ted could come too if he wished.

This morning, began to make a short list of some of my books, which Miss Coppen might be interested to buy. This gave me a sick feeling. However, the US Lines people inform me that I must procure an exit permit, and be ready to hand over my keys at the dock to the customs officials, as all baggage is now being examined before leaving the country. Anyhow, I couldn't carry books with me. It is better to get a little money for them if I can; but parting with my books, my specials, is like parting with my life's blood. However, better no books and America, than all my accumulated possessions in England forever. Indeed, I will be satisfied if I can get to America with nothing more than my life. To get home alive to America, Oh will it be possible?

- *SUNDAY, OCTOBER 22, 1939* -

In a private talk with Cuthie today he said he thought it would be better for me to stay in England. "I'd think you'd be better off here," he said. "Over there it's rotten. You'd always be sitting on somebody's doorstep. That would be horrid. Here you are your own boss, and maybe Dad will be different now we've gone."

Maybe he is right. He talked on some more about America, as he experienced it last year, and he kept on saying, "You wouldn't like it there, Ma. For a while it would be all right, but you wouldn't like living with any of the fellows. Better stay with Dad, I think."

Well, whatever the situation there would be, I don't know; but I'm certain that Cuth is positive I wouldn't like it, and that he wants me to stay here. Anyhow I have not yet heard from the Consul. I wrote to the consulate, asking for an interview, with the object of obtaining an immigration visa, last Sunday, the fifteenth.

- *THURSDAY, OCTOBER 24, 1939* -

I am going to the movies with Ted this evening. As we were returning, we were surprised to meet Artie, with Edna Renacre, at the bottom of Eastern Road.

Artie said he had been trying to burgle the house, but couldn't find a crack anywhere, to force an entrance. We all had a meal together, and then he had to leave for the nine seventeen train. He is in Old Chelsea Barracks, he says, amongst all the old red-coated pensioners, but he does not know for how long. He said he went to see his grandmother last night, and he will go again on Thursday. On Friday he is to be moved down into Kent somewhere. So Ted and I have arranged to go to Hammersmith also on Thursday, and say goodbye to him there.

- *THURSDAY, OCTOBER 26, 1939* -

Before we were out of bed this morning the telephone was ringing. It was Artie on the wire, saying he had longer leave than he expected, and he would be out to Romford about teatime. So he could have a hot bath, clean socks, etc., I had to send a wire to Mother, telling her she would have no Thompson visitors today. When he came, he brought Edna Renacre again, whom I thought a nuisance. He had to leave for the train, as he had to be at the Barracks before ten. They go down to camp somewhere near Canterbury tomorrow for eight weeks intensive training. Perhaps they'll have leave for Christmas, but this is not promised them. He has had no word from the R.A.F.

I am writing to both Gladys and Aileen. I wrote to them about two weeks ago, telling them about my decision to go to America. Today I wrote to tell them I had reversed my decision. Yesterday I received a parcel from Joan, containing a lovely embroidered tea cloth from her as a parting gift, and a silk tea cozy from Gladys. Somehow or other the reception of these gifts clarified my mind for me; I found I knew I wasn't going. I still have heard nothing from the Consul but now I don't need to hear. My mind is clear and steady; war or no war, husband or no husband, I'm going to stay here.

Ted did say something about me going in the week. He was asking what my plans were, and I told him I had not yet heard from the Consul. He was nice. Said he wanted to do what was the right thing for me, what was best for my happiness, but if he helped me to go it would still be against his wishes. He did not want me to go. Hadn't I better think it over some more? Wasn't I too impulsive? "Think about it some more, Lady, before you do anything rash, or anything that can't be easily undone." He kissed me with tenderness.

He was kind to me too on Sunday. The boys left here about five o'clock, to go to tea at the Pullan's, where there was a party, as Will was also home on leave. Cuth called a taxi, and as I watched them driving away, both in uniform, I felt I would die and I began to cry. Ted came over to me, and sat by me on the sofa, and put his arm around me, in comforting. Oh, why can't he always be kind? Why can't I remember his kind moments? Anyhow, I know now that I have decided to stay with him. I can't run away. We are married: for better for worse, 'til death do us part. God help me.

It is *The Feast of Christ the King*. Had it been a fine day I would have gone to mass. But it was a pouring wet morning so I didn't go out. Yesterday the new Pope published his first Evangelical. It will be known as Summi pontificatus, it's offering words. It analyzes "the radical and ultimate cause of the evils in modern society." This has led, step by step, to the present calamity of war. The condition of these errors is to be found in "the denial and rejection of a universal form of morality" through loss of belief in the Divinity of Christ and in God.

The two fundamental errors: "the forgetfulness of the law of human solidarity and Divine Charity" and "the divorce of civil authority from every kind of dependence on the Supreme Being." The civilization of the West cannot be restored, argues the Holy Father, except by the restoration of "the unity of doctrine, faith, customs and morals inculcated by the church." I agree. When the intelligence of the church speaks, I can assent to it, and though I have no feeling of faith, I can, with my head, acknowledge it as good and true. Ted's obstinacies, Mrs. Jude's superstitions, shouldn't keep me out of church, of course, they don't. They only keep me away from mass! I am a Catholic, willy-nilly. I can't help myself. So God help me!

EPISODE #5

- MONDAY, OCTOBER 30, 1939 -

I am feeling fine. Consequently have gone on a splurge and ordered half a dozen new books!

- SATURDAY, NOVEMBER 4, 1939 -

Old Herbert came in and brought us some enlargements of the snapshots of our boys, which had been taken on his terrace the other Sunday. They're very good photos. When he arrived, I was upstairs working on the bed for Cuthie, who had just phoned me about five p.m. that he would be home tonight, about midnight, and to leave the back door unbolted for him. I have had a very busy day, and no time to even look at my parcel of books, which Smith delivered at eight thirty this morning.

I forgot to note that our ration books arrived yesterday, though rationing is not to begin until next month.

- SATURDAY, NOVEMBER 11, 1939 -

Armistice Day

There is fresh trouble here in the Thompson family concerning the Arden Cottage group. Selma has quarreled with Mrs. Webb, the housekeeper, and her father has ordered her, Selma, to leave the house. The whole affair is sordid, and Bert's an imbecile. I think he's in his dotage.

- *MONDAY, NOVEMBER 15, 1939* -

The Selma trouble is getting worse, so I went out early this morning to see what I could do to mend matters, and to prevent worse happening. I called first on Mrs. How. My idea is to work up a campaign of talk to old Bert, from his friends, to get it into his head that he cannot act in the melodrama father manner and put Selma on the street.

Next I called in Dr. Donald; he told me that Selma goes to see him every Thursday, and she is quite friendly and rational towards him: that she has told him of her troubles regarding Mrs. Webb, and that her hands are now practically well. Her father and Mrs. Webb have accused her of poisoning them! She has had a touch of eczema on the backs of her hands so Bert and Mrs. Webb declared she poisoned everything she touched and made a great to-do about this. Donald simply laughs at their fears.

Next I called Peake's office, but did not see him. The office boy said he is away ill. So next I called the police station. I recognize that it is urgent to find out exactly what old Bert can do. There I received this advice: to see the doctor who knows this girl and to get a certificate that she is incapable of earning her own living, and with this to show that Herbert cannot throw the girl out. The law will compel him to support her. Also, to advise the girl not to leave her home, not to look for flats, not to take lodgings, not to move into a boarding house, but continue living her life at home in the normal way; and with this advice added that the father does not dare lay a hand on the girl to forcibly evict her, but in that case she could give him charge for assault.

Bert has suggested that Selma go and live in a bungalow at Chase Cross, in which Mrs. Webb's sister and brother-in-law now reside, and that this couple go to live with him in Arden Cottage! When old Bert put Selma out when he married Dorothy, it was a town scandal; but if he should put her out now because the housekeeper doesn't like her, and take the housekeeper's relations into his house in Selma's place, the scandal would be even greater; moreover, I think the town would judge that he was the nit-wit of the family.

- *THURSDAY, NOVEMBER 16, 1939* -

Old Bert was here to see me this afternoon. Ted has been talking to him, and now he came to me for my view on the situation. Naturally I have not told anybody of my Monday calls. Bert says Selma annoys him! What of it? Selma gets on everybody's nerves, sooner or later. He says he won't have her around, he abhors the sight of her, and he will have Mrs. Webb. We talked the whole afternoon, but I think all I have affected is a delay in his plans.

Watching Bert's conduct ever since Tillie died, and listening to his talk, I am filled with a complete disgust of the man. He has an idea he can do as he likes, and money will buy anything, and entitles him to whatever he fancies.

As I see it, Mrs. Webb is the usual common adventuress who sees in Bert easy money. I should say she has been deliberately stirring up trouble against Selma ever since she went into the house, with the direct aim of getting the girl out and the man to herself. Bert is the usual old fool, the usual lascivious old sensualist. He is going into his dotage. He's lost his wits, and the natural beast in him is clearly asserting itself. He's scared to death of the war, of illness, of dying, even of any inconvenience. Mrs. Webb consoles him! Moreover she is a good cook, a great virtue in his eyes, the greedy old fool! The fact that Selma is his daughter doesn't seem to register at all. As Ted pointed out, if he doesn't like his housekeeper he can dismiss her and go out into the open market and hire another, and keep on hiring and firing housekeepers until he does find a suitable one, but he can't send a daughter back for exchange. Bert is inhuman, and his absolute selfishness and egotism is past believing. He fills me with horror.

- FRIDAY, NOVEMBER 17, 1939 -

So tired and fed up with the family squabbles, I went off by myself to the movies this afternoon to find a distraction. The picture was an adaptation of *Wuthering Heights*, and I expected to enjoy it; instead, it bored me tremendously. The unreality of the whole story was fantastic; human beings, even in the wild Yorkshire moors, never behaved like these creatures of the mind. Of course it is not fair to judge a book by the movie made of it, and it is at least thirty years since I read the book. Nonetheless, if literature, as writing, evaporates on the screen, at least the plot, the situations, the characters of a book remain the pure story. Well, this story of *Wuthering Heights* is nonsense. Considering it as it is represented in its bare bones on the screen, it is obviously the absurd imaginations of a spinster, an uninitiated. No real men and women ever behaved as Emily Bronte imagined this group doing. Not one of them is alive, or ever was; they are palpably the ghouls evolved from the nostalgia and frustrations of a passionate and imaginative early Victorian spinster. Probably the book isn't even 'literature' in spite of the critics and the schools lauding it as such all these years.

Query: Can there be good writing about silly subjects? Can even a genius write convincingly about anything they do not know?

- *SUNDAY, NOVEMBER 19, 1939* -

The twins home for the weekend, on the same occasion again, which is surely unusual. They arrived for tea last night. Cuthie left soon after dinner today to go to the Newton's; Artie arrived at seven o'clock this evening. Artie expects to get his transfer into the Air Force about Christmas time; the proper officials have duly signed his papers, but he has to finish his eight weeks training course with the London Scottish before he will be transferred. He looks very well, but Cuthie is showing signs of nervousness, little facial twitches, reminiscent of Eddie.

- *MONDAY, NOVEMBER 20, 1939* -

A beautiful day; the best one we have had in six weeks. I went out walking most of the morning, and feel fine. Had some money to put in the bank for Cuth, and then walked up to Craig's and bought a two-drawer table I had seen there recently. It is of polished oak, fourteen inches by thirty inches with two deep drawers, and a handmade piece from Stones of Banbury. This is a gift for Cuth.

I got a telephone call from Miss Coppen before nine o'clock this morning, asking me to go to tea this afternoon and meet Mrs. Stanley Coppen. So called a taxi at three o'clock and went there. Talk fell upon a book all three of us had read within the last week. It is entitled *The Debate Continues: An autobiography of Margaret Campbell* (Marjorie Bowen).

Marjorie Bowen is a prolific authoress. Her first book, *The Viper of Milan,* was published when she was only seventeen years old. I remember when it came out. It was whilst I was in St. Martin's Le Grand, long before I was married, so I suppose I was still in my teens. I never read it. It was an historical novel and I seldom read historical novels, which are not to my taste. Naturally, I never followed up her work, but she established herself as a popular author. These later years she has turned to more serious work, a life and times of Hogarth, a life of John Wesley and, under the name of George Preedy, a Life of Mary Wollstonecraft and some other books which I have not seen. I read *Wrestling Jacob*, her life of John Wesley, when it first came out, a year or more ago, when there was a spate of books about the Wesley's, and I liked it immensely. It was a good book. Now comes her autobiography, and for the first time we learn "Marjorie Bowen" is only a pen name, and the real woman is named very differently, Margaret Campbell. Impossible to think of Marjorie Bowen as such, of course, but there's the fact.

Well, this 'Life' is morbid. It begins with the black unhappiness of the child, and ends with the accepted dull unhappiness of the elderly woman. It is some inherent defect in the woman, I think; for other children have been poor and had unsatisfactory relatives yet managed to extract happiness somewhere out of their lives; and other women have made mistaken marriages and lost an infant, and yet managed to be happy sometimes. In addition, Marjorie Bowen had a remunerative talent, which apparently never deserted her, once she had commercialized it, and yet she wasn't happy in her work. How extraordinary! If I could sell every book I could write, I don't think any catastrophe in the world could throw me into a pit of despair. I conclude that Marjorie Bowen is one of those unfortunate bores. Some people who can only be happy at being miserable.

- WEDNESDAY, NOVEMBER 22, 1939 -

Two new items added to the household today—Cuthie's table and a cat. Ted brought in a half Persian kitten today. I wonder if I am going to be able to tolerate it. Selma came in immediately after lunch, and stayed until nine thirty tonight. Now I'm a rag; she completely devitalizes me. I am sorry for the girl all right, but I wish she wouldn't fasten on me so much.

- FRIDAY, NOVEMBER 24, 1939 -

Old Bert and young Bertie came to see me this morning, and thoroughly depressed me. Not that they have anything against me, but to listen to their crassly materialistic conversation makes me feel absolutely ill. Not that young Bertie is so bad; he just naturally sides with his father. Old Bert is colossally selfish, and in his attitude towards all those people he doesn't like, he is downright inhuman. His attitude towards Selma is a positive disgrace. Ted says he is a pagan, but I think such a verdict maligns the pagans. Bert is selfish, gross, ill-bred, irreligious, and ignorant. Of course Selma is a fool; but she is his daughter all the same. Tonight I have the blues for fair.

At noon we had news that at eight o'clock this morning Russia invaded Finland, attacking simultaneously from land, air, and water. She had to protect herself from a lion. So now Finland is another victim of the Bolshevists and the Nazis. War spreads and spreads. During the last week our losses at sea have been very heavy, but serious fighting on the Western Front hasn't really begun yet. Where the end will be, God alone knows.

This morning I ordered books from Boots sale catalogue. I don't suppose I shall get all I asked for, but I'm bound to get a few bargains. Yes, I keep on buying books. I know it's a silly habit, but I still keep on doing it. Anyhow, I thank God that I can still read. If I couldn't escape somewhere from the agonies of this crazy world, how could I go on living in it?

EPISODE #6

- FRIDAY, DECEMBER 1, 1939 -

There is news this morning that the Finish Prime Minister resigned and a new cabinet is forming in Helsinki. Meanwhile, there is a lull in the Russian attack. I suppose Finland will have to accede to all of Russia's demands, or else be absolutely exterminated. Anyhow, Russia will swallow her, then, who next, the Scandinavian countries?

I received a queer complement this morning. I went out in mid-morning and crossed the bridge into Victoria Road; to go to Sam Gold's, the fishmonger. On my way back, an elderly woman walking with a cane accosted me.

"I must stop you," she said. "I saw you go down the street just now, and I said to my son, 'There's that woman. I want to go and speak to her.' I saw you once before, and I couldn't help noticing how sweet you looked, and I said to my son if I ever saw you again, I should have to speak to you. You have such a happy face. You look so contented, so well, so at peace. You look lovely. It's hard to walk against the wind isn't it? What is your trouble? Is it Arthritis? I have a stiff leg, it's quite set."

Of course I answered her; we stood and chatted a full ten minutes or more. She told me her name was Mrs. Green, she was sixty-eight years old, and she lived with her son, who had recently taken over The Chocolate Box.

She didn't look sixty-eight to me; perhaps enthusiasm keeps her young looking. When we parted, she squeezed my arm, and said, "Let's hope we meet again. You're lovely!"

Maybe she's a crazy woman. I don't know. What astonishes me is that she should think I looked happy and content. I should have thought that in repose my countenance had a melancholy cast. Apparently not. Apparently it still wears that faint smile of amiability, which appears in all my photographs, from childhood on. And peace, when I know no peace? That makes me remember Francis Burke saying to Patricia Saxton, "Don't you love it when Ruby visits you? When she comes into my house I feel all my troubles drop away. When Ruby comes in, peace comes in. Oh, she's so serene!" That didn't seem true then, but Patricia agreed that it was so.

Queer isn't it? My interior woman is forever in tumult; my soul is violent, yet my exterior is calm and calming, maybe because I pray for peace, for holy indifference, for serenity. To be serene; I suppose that is the deepest and most long abiding desire of my whole life. Apparently I have attained some sort of visible serenity. Queer.

- *THURSDAY, DECEMBER 21, 1939* -

It is the shortest day of the year. I am alone for the first time in weeks, and dreading to hear a knock at the door at any minute. I have been engaged very deeply in Selma's affairs. She refused to go to Worthington, as Bertie had arranged for her, so then old Bert said she would have to leave the house, as he positively would not have her in Arden Cottage. For days I had old Bert here twice and thrice a day, and Selma the same. They would both call on each other's heels, and Selma would sit in the kitchen and quake, and old Bert goes into the parlor to jaw. I consider him a first class bully. However, I finally found out that he would make her an allowance, though not until I had telephoned Peake, his solicitor. I would have taken the matter to court. As it was, I did go to the police station to find out exactly what he could do and couldn't do as he was threatening to practically put the girl out on the doorstep.

Then I had the job of flat hunting for the girl. Selma and I were out two days, looking for a suitable flat. Then I had a day with Bert, surveying some. He wanted to stick her up in Moss Lane, one of the Romford slums. Finally, I persuaded him to let her have a flat on this street, a new one, near the station.

If the girl has to live alone, as she had, position is very important, and she should be pleased with a good look-out, and very close to the main road. So she has gone into number twenty-two A. Taking up tenancy a week ago on the Eleventh, but then I had to supervise all the establishing, seeing about linens, blackout curtains, soap supplies, pots and pans, groceries of all sorts, coal and kindling, electricity, and so on. Bert shoved the job on me, but I made him pay for it, by stocking her up with enough of staple supplies to last her for three or four months. I was glad enough to do it for the girl. I think she has had a rough deal. Actually, she has been put out of her home to please the housekeeper, a Mrs. Webb, who presumably is no better than she should be. It is a fact that Selma is a selfish bore and a fool but she is old Bert's daughter just the same, and his action toward her is absolutely hateful and shameful.

Well, now she is settled, or we all hope she is. She still comes in to see me daily, and bores me to death with her silly talk; but once the holidays are out of the way, I shall tell her outright that I don't want her to come and see me every day. She must learn to live alone, and to manage her life for herself. She is a poor retarded introvert, but my God she is a plague to all who can't escape contact with her! Old Bert simply put her out. But that's a crime. What a likeness here to my Ted, both brothers arbitrarily arrange their lives to suit themselves, quite regardless of their children. Queer, isn't it?

Well, I have written the Christmas letters, made no Christmas preparations, read no books. I have been absolutely tired out with the Thompson affairs. We are going to be alone for Christmas. Neither of the boys will be able to be here. Artie who is training at Nutley, Sussex, will have leave from December 29th, to January 2nd. Cuthie, who is now with an operational squadron, stationed at Driffield, Yorkshire, does not expect to get any leave before March. I have written to Hammersmith and asked Mother to come and spend the Christmas with us, but so far have had no reply.

The war continues to get worse and worse. Finn's have not surrendered to Russia, and up to date are proving very successful fighters, but as there are about forty Russians to every Finn, I don't see how they can win in the long run. The war at sea is dreadful. The Germans are laying magnetic mines, and attaching neutrals. They bomb fishing boats from the air, and machine gun the fisherman on the decks, and in their little open boats.

Last week there was a big naval battle off South America, with the German pocket battleship, the Graf Spee. She was forced to take shelter in Montevideo Harbor, and when the Uruguayan Government declined to allow her to remain longer than seventy-two hours, she put to sea and sculled herself at the mouth of the River Plate. Yesterday came news of her commander; Captain Langsdorff had shot himself. This is all very inglorious. Also, yesterday, the German liner "Columbus" scuttled herself because she saw a British warship.

Christmas is safely past and we were alone for the day; the first time in all our lives that we have ever had Christmas alone together. It was nice, and we were happy. I'm still happy. This is very unusual for me; usually Christmas time depresses me horribly. This year, in spite of the awful wars, in spite of not having the boys, and they away soldiering, in spite of black fog, and no religion; nevertheless I was and am happy.

Our first Christmas together in America we spent with the Oberle's; our second with the Harvey's; our third was spent in Fortieth Street with Eddie in the crib, Mary Crowley in the kitchen, and Arthur Thompson arriving from Toronto just in time for dinner. There was a Mrs. Smith there, too, a Barbadian, whom Ted had invited because she had nowhere else to go, and there was an unborn infant there, too, as I was near my time with Harold. After that there were always children about, and visitors. And then here in England, the visitors again, at Arden Cottage, and since Tillie's death, we have made a Christmas again, for old Bert and Selma, Mother, and our twins. This year nobody was here.

Selma came in on Sunday, which was Christmas Eve, and stayed from three o'clock until ten thirty p.m. I wished her further. When she arrived she said her fire had gone out, so could she come to tea with us. Of course we had her but only because it was Christmas Eve, and we didn't want to hurt her feelings. Should she ever come with that excuse again, I shall tell her to go home and relight her fire. I have had that girl here every day for a month, or more, and I am heartily sick of her. However, we let her stay and kill Sunday.

The weather was awful, too. We had one of the blackest fogs we have had in years. Saturday was foggy, but Sunday was worse, and Christmas Day worse yet. Yesterday was foggy in the morning, but clearing at midday. Today, now the holiday is all over, we have sunshine again but it is very cold.

Artie surprised us by coming in about one o'clock on Sunday. He got a pass for the day. When evening came, he couldn't return. Neither buses nor trains were running. Nor could he hire a taxi. The fog was impenetrable, so about seven o'clock he returned to the house, and stayed here all night. This was very nice for Ted, as the two of them went to the 8 o'clock mass together on Christmas morning. Artie couldn't get a bus to Nutley until eleven o'clock so had time to have breakfast here. We expect him again on Friday, for a five-day leave, unless he is punished for not returning to headquarters on Sunday. He couldn't get there. It was one of the thickest fogs in years. On Christmas night, we heard in the news that a steamer from Jersey, which usually crossed the channel in six hours, had three nights on the water, with two hundred passengers aboard!

Yesterday, Boxing Day, the Jude's came to tea and spent the evening. It was all very jolly, and all had a good time. Today, we are going to the movies. I'm meeting Ted at five, at the Plaza, to see *Stanley and Livingstone,* Spencer Tracy as Stanley, and Sir Cedric Hardwicke as Livingstone. We didn't get to the movies last week. Nothing particularly attractive to us was offering, and as the weather was very disagreeable, we preferred the fireside.

It strikes me as we are going to hear some very bad news tonight. Our airplanes are going over constantly, bombers, in both directions, and flying very low. A group passed now which seemed almost to graze over our rooftops. There are many more about today than is usual, especially in this last hour.

Snow began falling about noon, and is continuing steadily, and there is a yellow darkness everywhere. All is very still, very cold, and very gloomy.

We expect Cuth home today, for a twelve-day leave, so if he is traveling down from Yorkshire today, he's going to have a beastly journey. I have just put two hot water bottles in his bed, and after tea, I will put some onions on to boil to make a nightcap for him. Artie is due home tomorrow, for a five-day leave. We got letters from him this morning. It appears he didn't get back to the barracks on Christmas Day after all. When he got to London on Christmas morning, he found there were no busses running and no train to East Grimstead until seven in the evening; so he went out to Hammersmith and ate a Christmas dinner with his Grandma. He writes she is as fit as a fiddle. When he did get to East Grimstead, he had an eight-mile walk, in the fog. However, he was excused his absence. It seemed that none of the fellows on leave with him were able to return, on account of the fog, but he was the last one of the lot to get in, being the one who had gone furthest a field. So, there were no punishments.

There was a severe earthquake in Turkey; between five and six thousand people killed in Anatolia. This world suffers one misery after another.

Letters arrived from America this morning. They have been on the way since December Eighth. New babies expected early in the year. Harold and Kay expect one in Christmas week, so that may be born already. Eddie and Chic expect their first in March, and Johnny and Ruth their fourth in January. This will bring the number of our grandchildren up to twelve. Incredible, but there it is.

I brought out an old photo of Grandma Searle this morning, to show to Mrs. Jude, who, of course, was calling. With Mrs. Jude and Selma, I never anymore get a day to myself. Mrs. Jude at once perceived a strong resemblance to me, in the picture. I can see it too. So, there's the Irish in me, for Grandma Searle was fifty-percent unadulterated Irish. She was the daughter of the infamous Joe Beate's. The damnable Irish!

- SATURDAY, DECEMBER 30, 1939 -

It is the last Saturday of the year. I am alone in the house. The boys at a dance at "The Kings Head", the Scottish New Year's Eve affair, which cannot be held tomorrow, that being Sunday, and Ted round at Bert's. Nine o'clock now, and in a few minutes I am going to make myself some sandwiches, and take them into the parlor, with a hot whiskey, to listen to Raymond Gram Swing from America, and the music that follows after. I have been writing and now I am tired.

When I got up this morning I was in a full flow of composition, with such an imperative urge to write, that I began jotting down before anyone came to breakfast. I have been writing in swatches on and off all day. I feel fine, and full of excitement, and of satisfaction. I am pleased with what I have done, and I feel I can continue in this strain. I haven't been able to write for months, but today the power began again with a rush, and I'm well away.

- WEDNESDAY, JANUARY 10, 1940 -

Mrs. Jude just left: then a chat with Miss Coppen on the telephone. The twins are twenty-one today. They were born just after the termination of the Great War; now they are fighting in this one. Artie was home for a few hours on

Sunday, but did not see Cuth, because he was spending the weekend with the Spaul's in Cambridge. Cuth returned to Driffield on Monday. Mother must have been the age I am now when the twins were born; if I live another twenty-one years, I shall be as old as mother is now, providing I also live so long. Time and time passing.

I was thirty-four when the twins were born, still a young woman. We were still in Bayonne. My God, I pray that long before another twenty-one years pass, I shall be living in Bayonne again! There's my home, there's where I can really rest in this world.

EPISODE #7

- FRIDAY, JANUARY 12, 1940 -

It is very cold, but a bright sun shining. I'm awfully happy. It isn't often I can say that, but today I'm happy. I am happy for no reason. Unless it is that the sun is shining. Anyhow, I have been less unhappy since the war started than for years before. I think it is because the war has given me Ted more to myself. He had to stop giving two nights a week to his damned Evidence Guild, because there was no longer a Guild he could devote himself to. With the outbreak of war, and the blackout, all street meetings and associations, all clubs, etc., automatically came to an end. Ted has even moderated his daily mass-going this winter, the first break in that peculiar regularity since we returned to England. This winter is proving a very severe one, and whether Ted doesn't feel too well, or whether laziness is encroaching on him, or whether at last his religious fervor is cooling, I don't know; but quite often in these last three months, three and even four mornings in the week, he has not gone out to the seven-thirty mass, but laid abed until eight o'clock. Marvelous!

It makes me feel good. I hate his religiousness, so when he forgets a little of it, my spirits lighten; he seems to me a more normal man, the kind of man I want.

When I woke this morning a refrain from "Elijah" was singing over and over again in my mind. It was from the solo "Oh Rest In The Lord," the line "and fret not thyself because of evildoers." It sang itself to me over and over again, and many times during the morning. I took it as good counsel, some word of guidance thrown up from my deep inner woman. I used to hear it at Swallow Street, of course, so it has lain with me all these years. Apparently nothing supersedes Swallow Street with me.

Well, yesterday I went to see Miss Coppen, who is laid up from the effects of a bad fall. It was thought at first that she had broken her thigh; but it is not broken only badly wrenched, muscle ligaments torn, and so on. Well, our talk ran on her sufferings; then on the horrors of the war; then on the affair of Selma and old Bert. There were a lot of condemnations, on which we mutually agreed together.

All was only with my head. As I observed myself, sitting there by her bed, I realized first of all that my sympathy with her was only society talk, and that my thought was that she exaggerated her mishap; then that her worry about the war was very personal, mostly fear for Maurice; then when I agreed with her as to what a hateful man Bert was, I found I really didn't care anymore. I know he is a sensual, selfish old beast but I simply don't care.

So this morning I feel that I can't worry about the war. I don't care a hoot about Hitler, Goring, Ribbentrop, and Company. I can't even care about the invasion of Finland, or the earthquake in Turkey. I just can't worry myself, that's what I feel.

The war is men's doing; the earthquake's natures, and I can't do anything about either. I'm just happy—unreasonably, unwarrantably happy. "And fret not thyself because of evil doers." It's not even because I am resting in The Lord. I'm not.

I think that Mother Nature really intended me to be a happy person, but events frustrated the plan. Many years ago, Ted once said to me, "The trouble with you is, that you want to be happy, that you expect to be happy, but there was no happiness promised to us in this world. This is a veil of tears, and the sooner you realize that, the better for you. The more you look for happiness, the more unhappy you're bound to be. You must reconcile yourself to the fact that there is no happiness in this world."

Like a fool, I believed him. That was a young husband talking! Of course there is happiness in this world, and I might have enjoyed it, much more than I have done, if I had believed in myself instead of in Ted and the hideous theology he was always dosing me with. Oh well, that's all gone by. I'm happy today anyhow. Happy.

- *SATURDAY, JANUARY 13, 1940* -

Ted left a few minutes ago for his evening of cards. I am furious with him, feeling downrightly that I hate him, and my hatred will never be assuaged. Of course I was too happy yesterday. I might have known it. In the evening, the nitwit Selma came calling, and stayed as usual until half past ten. A whole evening killed, scotched by a fool. She is beginning a habit of spending every Friday evening here. I won't have it. I've had more than enough of that girl to last me a lifetime. I won't let her use up one evening a week of my precious time. Ted, of course, was sweet to her. I wasn't rude, of course, but he was saccharine until he got tired of her clatter, when he then took up a book. She's his niece, therefore, perfect!

This morning trouble arose. We had a downright quarrel and so far I've been feeling full of hatred and irritation all day, and now I'm tired out with it.

Ted lay abed until half past ten, and when he came down to breakfast he began asking me a series of questions about the stopped up waste pipe in the lavatory basin. We are having a very severe cold spell, and pipes are freezing. When I went to the bathroom last night, I found the basin full of hot water. Ted's idea of heating the bathroom! All it does of course is to steam the walls; this water then condenses and freezes on the ceiling, and when a thaw comes, it falls in pools on the floor. This is one of Ted's bright ideas! Well, I let the water out of the basin, and left the plug in, because the tap drips and the drips collect and freezes in the pipe if it is not plugged. When I went into wash this morning, the water was running from the tap all right, but the waste pipe was frozen up again, and I could not let my water out.

Well, when Ted came downstairs, he asked a dozen questions about it, and when I had answered them all, he asked them all again. I answered them again, his usual manner of cross-questioning. I got exasperated and answered shortly. This huffed him, and he read me a lecture on manners and the faults of my character in general. I replied that I didn't mind answering straightforward questions, but I hated to keep on answering the same questions over and over. Then he said I interrupted him, which was very rude, and I shouldn't do it, not even to a grocery boy! Then he told me I was like my mother and went on and on. I said, "Shut up!" This took him into a homily about 'goodness', and according to him I was deficient in goodness. I just got bored and more bored.

Upon my word, the more often I have to listen to Ted, the bigger fool I think him. He has been particularly trying along the holidays. Having the boys at home seems to set him off. He talks to them and to me as though we were all children, youngsters in the kindergarten, to whom he must explain a whole lot of things. He expounded the obvious until we all grew restive. Or he was humorous in the silly, facetious manner of an adolescent. The boys were polite but bored, as I'm always bored by what he thinks are his jokes. Actually, Ted has just as much of an arrested mind as Selma has. The only advantage is that he got to know a little more before his mind stopped. It is stopped. He is as much of a dead ender as she is. Bert, it's the rotten sop Thompson mind.

At eleven thirty Ted went out, and I went up to tidy the bedroom. Then when I came to make the bed I found that he had been having emissions. The sheet was soiled in several places, and his pajamas stiff with dried semen. So that's why he was so cross—nature denied. I suppose he had been dreaming of one of his lady friends. This afternoon he went out to confession. What a fool he is, what a God damned fool! When he came in at lunchtime, he went straight to the radio and turned it off. It was playing dance music. Naturally, he doesn't approve of that. There was no by your leave, or any of that, no inquiry as to did I wish to listen. Oh no, he doesn't like it, and that was that.

After lunch we got the first act of Madame Butterfly from Saddlers Wells Theater. I stayed in the kitchen, to hear it in peace, but he sulked alone in the parlor. Silly fool! I thought to myself, how we waste life, and our opportunities of pleasure! Ted and I haven't been to a theatre for years. We haven't been out together anywhere since New Year's, a year ago, when we had to go to the Consulate. We could have pleasant times together. We could take in a theater and dinner in town at least once a month. We could make excursions. We could run a motorcar. We could take holidays together. But no, none of this ever happens. All we ever do is go to the movies together about once a week—never more than one a week—and some weeks not at all. We meet in the foyer, and we sit in the shilling seats, and all the way home Ted talks about how silly the pictures are. Preposterous, isn't it? We never visit anywhere; we never ever take a walk together. What a life! What a silly, silly life!

No sensible person ever comes to the house. All we get are fool women. No man at all comes here, except occasionally old Bert. Bert's no asset. He's ignorant and gross. God, my Thompson in-laws! It's only because they are in-laws that they ever get in at all; otherwise I wouldn't even open the door to them. Ted and Bert and Selma, they're all fools together. Ted did have brains once, but they grow softer and softer. Oh he does bore me! God! Will marriage ever end?

- *JANUARY 14, 1940* -

It is still very cold, but our dispositions more clement. This is Charlie's birthday; he is twenty-six today. I have been plunged in dreams of Bayonne all day. I think, in fancy. I have walked every street and every avenue, noted every house, shop, church, school, theatre, and shack, sat on 35th Street Station and watched the trains and the harbor, and chatted with every old friend. Bayonne. It was there the best years of my life were lived, and it is there I will go back. Thinking about this intention, alone in the dusk, whilst Ted was at Benediction, and wondering whether I couldn't coerce it by my will into actuality, compel it to realize, suddenly I thought, I will pray for it! The gospel promises flashed into my mind, and all at once I found I could believe them! I say that he that shall not doubt in his heart, but shall believe that what he saith cometh to pass: he shall have it. Therefore I say unto you, all things whatsoever ye pray and ask for, believe that ye have received them, and ye shall have them.

So, I do believe that I will get back there, back to Bayonne. I do see myself living there in peace and thankfulness, and I do pray and ask for it. I will pray for it every day. Give me my Bayonne home, dear Jesus, for thy name's sake, for thy Father's sake, God, take me home to Bayonne, for Jesus Christ's sake. Amen.

- *MONDAY, JANUARY 15, 1940* -

When I wakened this morning my inner woman was saying, very clearly: I go fishing. I go a-fishing. This didn't seem to make sense, yet somehow the phrase was familiar. During the morning it came to me what it was. It was what St. Peter said one day to his friends, one day after the resurrection, and his friend's said, "If you go, we will go with you," and it was when they returned from the night's take that they found Jesus on the shore, with a fire burning and a fish broiling, and they all had breakfast together.

What did the phrase mean for me? The same I think that it meant for Peter; that we must get on with our jobs no matter what events shake us, what disappointments cast us down, what hopes are dashed, what glories fade, we must proceed with our lives according to the necessities laid upon them. Peter was a fisherman, catastrophe had overtaken him, but he had to go on living, and he lived by following the calling of a fisherman. "I go a-fishing." So with me, and the job I must do…I go a-fishing.

- *FRIDAY, JANUARY 26, 1940* -

Snow is falling again. This is proving an extraordinarily severe winter. Not only here in England, but all over

Europe and also Northern America. Everybody suffers from the inclemency of the weather, but actually it is proving a blessing, because it holds up most war maneuvers, particularly in Finland, where it definitely helps the Finns and defeats the Russians. The Russians are being frozen to death!

- *MONDAY, JANUARY 29, 1940* -

The weather is abominable. Yesterday London had twenty-seven degrees of frost. Today must be even colder, for a gale is blowing from the North. This is the coldest winter in England, they say, since eighteen ninety-four. Snow around here is more than a foot deep and much deeper in places where the wind has piled it. Nevertheless, Ted gets up mornings and goes out to mass. The funny thing is, he doesn't catch cold. You can't tell me this is piety. I think it is the strength of habit, and the folly of a fool. In the house he is thoroughly disagreeable; he finds fault with everything, then returns to the parlor to read a book entitled, *The Love of God*. What a man!

Yesterday we had a downright quarrel. As usual, I spent the morning cooking dinner. It was roast leg of pork, applesauce, parsnips, potatoes, and peas, with pineapple salad, and coffee and cakes. Bakery cakes: fancies. When Ted came to the table he said I had put too much gravy on his plate, so it had taken away his appetite, and he practically ate nothing. Now, nothing annoys a cook so much as to have her good meal disregarded; she feels she might have saved her trouble, and wishes she had. This was the third meal running that Ted had found fault with! At breakfast he had complained of the bacon, that was cut too thin and not fried right, and on Saturday night, he complained of the fried fish I gave him. That was too dry.

Well, I ate my dinner, and said nothing. But I made up my mind I wouldn't eat tea with him. He could eat that alone.

We sat together in the parlor until three thirty when he went out to church again. Neither weather nor temper made any difference to him; to church he would go, so he went. I listened to the wireless, and continued to listen to all I wanted to hear, which was until half past six. Then I came to the back regions, laid the table, made some tea, cut some sandwiches, and put out a bowl of cold jellied consommé for him. My intention was to eat my tea, then retire to the parlor whilst he came to the table. Before I could begin, there was a knock at the door, and lo, it was Selma! Ted came to the kitchen to tell me. In a moment I flared into anger. Another fool Thompson was more than I could stand. I said, "Take her in the parlor, then, and entertain her. She's your niece."

"No, I see she's just in time to share a meal. I shall bring her out here."

"I don't want to see the girl. I am sick of the sight of her."

"Too bad! I shall bring her into tea just the same."

"If you do, I'll walk out of the room!"

He went away, and the two of them shut themselves into the parlor. I put my sandwiches onto a plate, ready to carry them away if he brought her to table. I drank a cup of tea. Then I heard footsteps in the passage, a knock at the door. I didn't reply. Another knock. I didn't reply. Then the damn fool girl opened the door, and began piping, "Oh, Auntie, I only just wanted …" All beams and smiles. I spilled over. I shouted at her, "Selma, don't you understand? I don't want to see you! Your uncle and I are quarreling like hell, and I don't want any more Thompson's around. I'm sick of the sight of the whole lot of you. I say, damn the Thompson's. Go away. Go away! Goodnight. Goodnight, Selma! Shut the door. Shut the door and go away!" So she retreated. Presently the front door banged; she'd gone.

Then Ted came in, and sat down to his cold consommé. We ate in silence. I was wrong, of course. I know that. I am sick of Selma. I am sick of the Thompson's. Old Bert is a fool, Selma's a fool, and Ted's a fool. I weary to death of all of them. Selma is one confounded nuisance. She's always on the doorstep. She wants to visit, so she visits. I've had enough of her, too much of her. I was glad enough to help her when her father threw her out, but I'm not holding her in my lap for the rest of time. She is one colossal bore and she won't bore me any longer. In the future I will save my feelings, not hers, and if she can't make sense when she isn't welcome, she'll be brutally told when so. If I had a maid to answer my door, Selma would have been barricaded out years ago. Dear little Selma, of course, can do no wrong; why, she's a Thompson! I say curse the Thompson's.

EPISODE #8

- WEDNESDAY, JANUARY 31, 1940 -

The thaw. I am expecting Artie in this evening for a week's leave, but whether he can get here is doubtful. For several days now all transport, rail and road, has been disorganized or not working at all. Yesterday a train from Glasgow arrived at Euston twenty-eight hours late. The cold has been intense here in London; we were down to twenty-nine degrees of frost and the snowfall heavy. On Monday the Radioman told me that at Upminster he couldn't get through at all; the snow was five feet deep. Neither milk nor coal get into towns, and outlying villages in Derbyshire, Buxton, and Lanshire have been completely cut off from the world for over three days, and are running out of all food supplies. England hasn't had a winter like this, the weathermen say, since eighteen ninety-four. The Thames at Surbiton and Teddington is frozen over for eight miles. The serpentine, of course, where there is gala-skating going on. The Transport Board reports that they have no such difficulties on record. So it is the worst ever. Of course with the thaw we shall get floods. The sky right now looks as though it will let down another heavy snowfall by night.

Anyhow, the temperature has moderated, so tempers have improved quite a bit. So that's lucky. Mrs. Shaw should have been here today but didn't show up. I'm not surprised. The roads are practically impassable. I wouldn't go out either.

I'm sitting down to a re-reading of *Saints, Sinners, and Beecher's*. I dream persistently of Bayonne, of America, and now this blizzard weather particularly sets me to daydreaming of American winters. So I feel I'll browse with the Beecher's for an hour or two. Au-Revoir.

- *MONDAY, FEBRUARY 5, 1940* -

For a week or more I have had a vision of the corner of East Thirty-Third Street and Broadway, Bayonne, in my mind's eye, and nothing would shift it. I had a dream that I was standing on that corner, outside the First National Bank, talking to Mrs. Hewetson, and the thawed snow was roaring down the corner gutter. I had a baby in a baby carriage. She was holding the small Jackie by the hand. It was a picture of thirty years ago. We were young, as we were. Now today the picture has been displaced by one of the Bayonne Library steps.

Another dream. It is still the thawing season, and the wooden steps are in place in the center of the great steps. They were sopping wet and I am walking up the wet stone steps beside them. The library door is open; overhead the sky is a gorgeous clear blue. A dream, more real to me than the English room in which I am at the moment sitting. My Bayonne, my America, my home. It is true: only the lost is one's forever.

I am not exactly homesick, but I am not here. I have been reading old American books, to hold the scene, to keep the atmosphere. Reading about the Beecher's, the Gothic American. Mrs. Eddy. This morning, I read haphazardly in *Science and Health*. It is better than I remembered it. It's a hodge-podge—she's a plagiarist—but she was certainly saying something. Even if she was a plagiarist, she nevertheless had the wit and the stick-at-it-ness to make a fine bouquet of her own from the blooms she had gathered from other people's gardens. It is her bouquet which is a concrete thing, which works, and which lasts.

I read Fisher's book about her last week. His greatest grievance about her teaching (apart from his sneers at her life) is that she takes all personality away from God. To me, that is one of her great achievements. To me, the personality of God, especially the masculine personality of God, is always a stumbling block. Mrs. Eddy has annihilated that. She presents God as truth, life, love, mind, and principle.

After all, didn't Jesus say, "I am the Way, the Truth, and the Life?" Didn't he say, "God is spirit?" St John, "God is Love?" It is in these terms I can think of God. God as a person, as a He? No, I cannot.

This is a dull day, inclined to be foggy. Artie has gone to town for the day, and Edna Renacre has gone with him. I wonder if this friendship is going to become an engagement. Although Edna is a really nice girl, I hope not. Artie is too young for that, and the war is too troubling. This war may drag on for years yet, and then, when it's all over, Artie will have no work, no prospects. To get engaged now is to tie his hands. The girl is persistent, and she may persuade him that he is "in love". I do hope not. I want Artie to keep free until he has discovered just exactly what he wants to do with his life. Merely to become a husband is not much. Though, of course, to become a wife is a girl's end of scheming.

- TUESDAY, FEBRUARY 6, 1940 -

It is Shrove Tuesday, but no pancakes. Mrs. Jude here to lunch; at teatime, only Ted and me. So, as we were full of pudding, decided it was too bothersome to make pancakes, just for we two.

Mrs. Jude has a brand new prophecy. One of the sisters of the Little Flower died this week. Mrs. Jude tells me that before she died the Little Flower appeared to her, and told her that the war would be all over in two months from her death.

"Now that was a fort-night ago," Mrs. Jude said. "She's been dead just two weeks. You'll see, in another two months the war will be all over. The Little Flower said so!"

Yes. We will see all right. Mrs. Jude is the most absolutely superstitious person I have ever come across. There is no talk of wonders too difficult for her to swallow.

- WEDNESDAY, FEBRUARY 7, 1940 -

Ash Wednesday

Artie returned to the barracks today, but there is a chance he may be home again for the weekend. Mrs. Jude was here again today. I suppose she is having one of her spasms of visiting. I showed her a letter in the *Times*, which pleased her. Somebody wrote in to draw attention to a prophecy in Daniel Eleven. It is from Verse twenty-one, and on. It really is a very appropriate description of Hitler and Hitler's doings. It really is remarkable.

At eleven o'clock this morning the air raid warning sounded. It was only a practice signal, which it has been arranged to sound at eleven o'clock in the morning of every first Wednesday of the month; but one forgets this, or what day of the month it is, and when the warning siren goes off, one suffers a panic, willy-nilly. Suddenly I felt as though I had no insides, and probably a siren sounding will do that to me for the rest of my life.

TO THE EDITOR OF THE *TIMES*, WEDNESDAY, FEBRUARY 7, 1940

A Prophecy from Daniel

"Sir, you have published in your columns two extracts from Jeremiah and from Ezra's, which appear to be prophetic of current events. In the eleventh chapter of the Book of Daniel (verse twenty-one) I extract the following description, which appears particularly applicable to the Fuhrer, indicating his views and aims and destined fate."

"And in his place shall stand up a contemptible person to whom they had not given the honor of the Kingdom, but he shall come in time of security, and shall obtain the Kingdom by flatteries. And with the arms of a flood shall they be swept away from before him and shall be broken.

"And after the league made with him he shall work deceitfully; for he shall come up and shall become strong with a small people. In time of security shall he come even upon the farthest places of the province; and he shall do that which his fathers have not done, nor his fathers' fathers; he shall scatter among them prey and spoil and substance: yea he shall devise his devices against the strongholds even for a time...

"And the King shall do accordingly to his will; and he shall exalt himself and magnify himself above every god, and shall speak marvelous things against the God of gods

and he shall prosper 'til the indignation be accomplished; for that which is determined shall be done.

"Neither shall he regard the gods of his fathers, nor the desire of women, nor any god: for he shall magnify himself above all. But in his place shall he honor the god of fortresses."

Yours, & c., A. Wigglesworth. Port of London Building, Trinity Square

- *THURSDAY, FEBRUARY 8, 1940* -

I had Mrs. Bull in to see me this morning. When Ted came into dinner yesterday, he told us that he had heard a conversation between Mrs. Bull and old Bert, in the office, from which it appeared that old Bert had written her a letter (why write? except that he couldn't face her) laying her off from her job of cleaning the office. It seems she has cleaned the office for twenty-nine years, and she wanted to know why she was dismissed so summarily. I gathered, too, that she had quit at Arden Cottage. So I wrote her in the afternoon, and asked her did she want to resume my work; Mrs. Shaw resigned the job last week, as she is ill.

So Mrs. Bull came to see me this morning, and I got an earful. It appears she hasn't technically "left" her job at Arden Cottage but is on the panel, as she is so tired she had to see the doctor, and he has ordered her to rest. Nevertheless, her daughter, who frequently helps her with that job, did her office cleaning for her. She only quit working for me because Bert persuaded her to give all her time to him, at Arden Cottage, and I agreed because of the domestic upheavals there, since the death of Tillie. Well, I heard some weeks ago that old Bert was bullying Mrs.

Bull to make her give up her ration cards to him; but this she refused to do. Quite naturally she preferred to use her rations in her home with her daughter. Bert thought he ought to have them, and even talked about going to see the Food Controller about them. Much good that would have done him. One's rations are one's own, and certainly do not have to be surrendered by a daily worker to her employer. Why should they? If Mrs. Bull's ration of meat went into the Arden Cottage joint, what would she get? The joint would go into the dining room, and after old Bert and Mrs. Webb had had first cuts, Mrs. Bull could have the leavings. Of course that isn't good enough. Further, as Mrs. Bull naturally asks: What about Mrs. Webb's relations ration-cards? Why not ask for them, since her relations are so frequently at Arden Cottage?

Mrs. Bull tells me that Mrs. Webb's relations—two sisters, a brother, and a brother-in-law—are sponging on old Bert practically all the time. They come every evening, every Sunday, the sisters are there all day, and often they all sleep there. They booze, at Bert's expense. Mrs. Webb is frequently the worse for drink, and slobbers over Bert.

"Kisses him, Mrs. Thompson," Mrs. Bull said, "it's disgusting. She sits in the dining room, so bold. Her skirts pulled right up, and old Mr. Bert looking at her legs. I've seen him. The hussy, that's all she is. I can't stand it, Mrs. Thompson. That's why I'm so tired. That's why I'm run down. It worries me. Mr. Thompson says it's my own fault, because I won't sleep in there. I can't. I did try it. I can't settle in that house. It's horrible with that Mrs. Webb there."

So she's on sick leave; but to be further unpleasant old Bert is now holding up her insurance card! He is a disagreeable cantankerous old beast. So the next move is to sack her from the office job. Of course this is Mrs.

Webb's instigation; only a woman would think of such a trick.

Also, I hear that old Bert is scared to death of Mrs. Webb's husband. Mrs. Bull says he watches the house and walks around it at night, so, every time they hear a footstep after dark, old Bert gets in a dither.

"You can see him," said Mrs. Bull. "He's as nervous as a cat."

I should think he would be. He'll find himself sued, or appearing as a co-respondent in the divorce courts yet. I wonder what young Bertie thinks of it all. Old Bert has developed into a boozy lecherous beast, an inhuman father, a disgrace to his family, and a scandal to the town. He's another old fellow who has lived too long. Of course this core of badness, this crass selfishness and bestiality, must have always been in him. It was Tillie that kept it in check. With Tillie gone, the real man appears, and it is a disgusting and valueless man.

- *FRIDAY, FEBRUARY 9, 1940* -

I had a busy morning pastry making, but thinking all the time about old Bert, and the Thompson family, generally.

I never knew my parents-in-law, but they must have been poor stuff. Tillie told me something about them. When she came from America as a bride, in 1900, she and Bert took a house beside their house, so she knew both of them from that time until they died. Her opinion was that Mrs. Thompson had the better brains and character of the pair, and that it was she who ruled the family, and kept it together. In a way, she thought the mother was too good to the father. The father, I gathered, was an easygoing master, and an old soak. Tillie also told me about the crazy grandmother, as Grace had done, when in New York. I have an ever deepening conviction that the Thompson's are, and were, all mad, in some degree or another, or, if not mad, something short in their brain box, sort of ten pence-halfpenny in the shilling, as it were. Certainly I am convinced that if I had ever met any of Ted's people before I married him, I never should have married him. I should have seen at once that they were definitely not my kind of people, and I should have left them to their East End, where they obviously and naturally belonged. The fact that the younger children went up in the world was a fluke, as the fact that the younger ones had brains was a fluke. Bert hasn't got brains; he's only had luck. It was the last war made his money for him. Young Bertie gets his brains from his mother; Tillie had no education to speak of, but she was a very smart woman with a good wit; as for Selma, she is probably a throwback to the Grandmother, born a moron, and now definitely cracked, going loony because of sex frustration.

Old Bert's conduct since the death of Tillie has been one absurd escapade after another. Of course he's scared of dying, and most of his silly actions have been attempts to cheat old age and closer coming death. I guess he has always been afraid of dying, and always running away from difficulties. When he went to the Klondike, he was running away from his first wife; and when he became sick up there in Alaska, he turned tail at once and ran out of it, leaving my Ted, a lad of only eighteen, to shift for himself. That was a dirty deal too. Well, I suppose he will soon be running away from Mrs. Webb, unless death cops him soon.

I wonder about my own children. What dab of the bunch have they got? Nobody could ever be saner than a Searle or a Side, and I'm sure I'm no fool as the world recognizes fools. As for Ted, I think he is a fool, and I think he grows more foolish as time proceeds. Practically daily now, as I listen to his silly talk, my exasperated and impatient inner woman is secretly exclaiming at him, “Oh you bloody fool!” As for the conduct of his life, what could have been more fantastic and unbalanced? As for his religion, what is there normal and sane about that? This is a man who was clever in his youth, a man who achieved education and culture and climbed to the top of the ladder, but now where is he and what is he? Today he’s a poor sap, now here. He’s reverted to an original Thompson, a plebian crackpot.

EPISODE #9

- MONDAY, FEBRUARY 12, 1940 -

I went out today for the first time this year. The cold has been deep, and we've had more snow. Very cold indeed this morning, but the roads were clear, so I decided to go out. I put some money in the bank for Cuthie, and then went to Stone's. I bought three blousettes to wear with my Barker dress, and some silk and lavender wool to knit myself a vest. There is one thing this severe winter has showed me, that I haven't got proper under clothes for a severe cold snap. My American "Athena's" are all worn out, and the combs I bought at Selfridge's are very ill fitting. I don't possess one flannel petticoat. Therefore I am determined to have proper lightweight woolen under things before next winter comes around. I bought the velvet wool as a start but principally as a change from the knitting of socks, of which job I have become very tired.

The blousettes were needed, though of course I didn't need three. One would have done. However, I saw them and liked them, so I bought them. I am determined to have nice clothes.

When I came out of the store, I found snow had begun falling again, and everything was already thickly covered. I found walking perilous, and nearly fell. A policeman came to the rescue, and called a taxi for me.

I am reading Aldous Huxley's, *After Many a Summer,* and liking it.

- FRIDAY, FEBRUARY 16, 1940 -

More snow. Ted has a very bad cold. At ten thirty p.m. the telephone rang. Ted answered it promptly. We thought it might be Cuthie giving us a night call. But no, it was Mary Bernadette. Ted gave monosyllabic answers, and when he hung up, he swore. That girl had asked him to let her Mother know that she wouldn't be home until about eleven thirty p.m. Taken by surprise, Ted had agreed; he had been just about ready for bed, sitting over the fire all evening in his dressing gown, and with his slippers on. So he had to dress and go up past Carlton Road to give Mrs. Jude, Mary's message. What impudence! This girl of twenty calls up an elderly man, late at night, to run a message for her; and what a message, merely to tell her mother she was delayed an hour. Cheek!

Anyhow, the Jude's are a general nuisance about the telephone. Mrs. Jude will not install one of their own, because she won't pay for it, but she makes a convenience of all the neighbors. She has exhausted the goodwill of the Dumaresque's about it and now she has exhausted ours.

When Mary was in training in the hospital, she would ring up at any time she wished, and ask Artie to take messages to her mother for her. Now she has rung up Artie's father, and late at night, too! That's a colossal impertinence. Mrs. Jude comes here whenever she wishes to ring up Mary in town; moreover, to have me ring up Mary's office for her, and make excuses for her absences. Further, when Mrs. Jude is visiting here, sometimes the telephone will ring, and she will say "oh-that's my Mary. I told her to call me up here this afternoon." Off she rushes to answer the phone. Never a by your leave, or a thank you; they have arranged this convenience, and I can put up with it.

Mrs. Jude was here at teatime last Saturday, to call up Mary at John Kavanaugh's, and she had Ted do the actual calling! Never does she offer to pay for a call, never once has she made an offer to pay.

Well that's how some people get by; they manage to use all the luxuries of life, at other people's expense. "Grafters" we call them in America, and that term exactly describes them.

- *SUNDAY, FEBRUARY 18, 1940* -

I made a chicken dinner today, with corn pudding as the accompaniment, and vanilla custard to follow as the nearest approach I can get in England to ice cream. The boys won't eat chicken, but now they are not here, there is no reason why Ted and I shouldn't eat chicken sometimes.

The American Sunday dinner: fried chicken and corn fritters with ice cream and cake for dessert.

- *MONDAY, FEBRUARY 19, 1940* -

I am restless and homesick. I spent most of the afternoon and evening turning through my American cookbooks and notebooks and old files of the *Rural New-Yorker*. Queer how American cookbooks serve me as an anodyne! Just to read about corn bread and apple dowdy, clam chowder and Washington pie, can calm me. I have Eve Curie's Life of her mother, *Marie Curie*, on hand, and am enjoying it rather. It is a very long book, so I am wearying of it a little. Probably it is this book which has disturbed me. Marie Curie, who lived the life of an exile, and for whom life never turned out as she wished it to be, it's a sad story, and it saddens me; not because I am sympathetic to Marie's woes—I'm not, I'm not "sympathetic" at all, I'm not that sort of person—but because, in spite of everything, Marie achieved her intentions; and I achieve nothing. That is my trouble. To read of such a successful life jolts me into an intolerable awareness of my own failure.

- *TUESDAY, FEBRUARY 20, 1940* -

Rains, so it is warmer, thank heaven. Ted made an acute remark this morning. We were dawdling over breakfast, talking about the news and the Germans, and I remarked that I had been dreaming about the Salzmann's and their bakery on Thirty-Fourth Street, in Bayonne. We reminisced about Salzmann's a bit, and then Ted said, "You know, you are a funny one. In art and politics, and styles and ideas, you're so modern, or think you are. You hate repetitions; you want everything new; yet in your real life you are an absolute conservative. Anyone to hear you talk about the past—why, you even dream about it!—would never credit you as a modernist. Why, in your mind, you live before two wars!"

What he says is true. That's where my heart is. As Ted said, I've lived here in Romford for a dozen years and yet I'm never really here at all. It's true, I'm not. I have no care for anything here in Romford, or anywhere here in all England. Every place is only something temporary to me. I feel a stranger, an exile, a transient, all the time. I am a stranger, an exile, and a transient. I'm waiting, all the time, to go back home. My home is in America. I want to pick up my life where it was truncated, and to put joy and vitality and satisfaction into it once again. Satisfaction. I want to be satisfied. Isn't there an expression in the scriptures somewhere "then I shall be satisfied?" Well, when? When I open my door in Bayonne once again.

- WEDNESDAY, FEBRUARY 21, 1940 -

Johnny's birthday. He is thirty today.

- THURSDAY, FEBRUARY 22, 1940 -

Washington's Birthday

I awoke this morning from a vivid dream of Will Watson. Why? Why Will Watson out of all the ghosts of the past? He was real as he was real forty years ago. He was standing in Mother's kitchen as he used to stand: tall, handsome, smiling, and mocking, exuberantly alive, and filling me with an ecstasy, as his presence always used to do. Why?

Trying to find the association of thought in my waking life which threw him up so vividly into my dream life, I think became right out of my reading of the life of Madame Curie. Deviously, but I think like this: Marie Curie was an essentially lonely woman, but she kept to the end of her life a very deep love and friendship with her sisters and brother, and when in old age one sister was devastated by the loss of her husband and her children, Marie consoled her by writing that she still had her sister and brother with her, at least the three of them were alive together, in Warsaw.

I think it is this fidelity and ever-lasting love in friendship, which was the rock jutting into my old subconscious. I am a woman, for whom circumstances have destroyed friendships, but I crave friendship and there is never a friend. For my parents there were always friends, and their friendships were indestructible. They quarreled with each other, but they never quarreled with their friends. Both of them kept their friends to the grave. The boys and girls they grew up with, the young couples they became intimate with in their own young married life, their brothers and sisters and cousins, nobody once in the circle was ever dropped out. Our house was open to all, in good fortune or bad, in fun or in sorrow, in youth and in age, all sorts of people came and went: friends.

Partners die. The widowed remarry. It is all the same to my mother and father. Newcomers to other families are welcomed into ours. Friends are loved, received and visited, until the grave. I can remember scores of the friends who came into Angel Road, and not one of them was ever dropped.

The Watson's were a family who lived in Notting Hill during the seventies. The father kept a barbershop, and his three sons, Will, Harry, and Fred, were all his lather boys. They were boys with Dad. The father died, and as the mother could not carry on a barber's business, and the boys were too young to do so, she exchanged the barber shop for a stationers and newsagents. Harry used to peddle magazines for her, until he succeeded getting into the District Railway offices with Dad. Will took up with engineering. Fred ran away and enlisted in the army. Unable to carry on her shop alone, Mrs. Watson took up mid-wifery, and she acted as midwife for my mother when I was born. She only lived for a few years longer, but I can remember her.

Will and Harry were very partial to Dad, and were often in our house. Harry married a schoolteacher and went to live in Galing, so visiting was easy. Will married his cousin, a woman older than himself, and who turned out to be a dipsomaniac. They lived in Wantage, where Will had charge of a small tramline. Young Willie Watson, a boy about my age, and their only child, was one of the trials of my childhood. He came to live with us once, some period whilst his mother was under restraint. He was a wildish, untrained boy, and as I had no brothers, I found him a great tease and nuisance. From Wantage, every now and then, Will Watson would come and stay with us in Angel Road, and then there came a time when he stayed for several months. There had been a scandal in Wantage, with Mrs. Watson drinking, and Will carrying on with a famous lady cricketer, so he had lost his job and came to London to look for work. Mother and Dad took him in, just naturally he stayed with us for some months, until he found a job. He finally got a job as inspector on the new Two-Penny Tube, which had just opened, and then he took rooms in Shepherds Bush somewhere. He kept his inspector ship for some years, but finally became ill, and died of T.B. His son, like me, now become an elderly person, is still faithful to Angel Road, and every now and then pays a call on Mother. So I think it was that faithfulness my soul was seeking.

My parents didn't care when Will Watson was in disgrace and had lost his job; they took him in the same as ever; they were friends. That's what I want: faithful friendship. I live in most terrible isolation. I have been writing to the American Consul this week. I had a letter from the Consulate on the twelfth about my visa, and offering an appointment. I have been in a certain distress ever since, but at last I answered it, and said I was withdrawing my request for a visa, for the present. So that disturbs me. In memory, all my American life is churned up, and I am homesick, homesick and I cannot go home. I want my American children, my American friends, and I must continue to want.

Once in these last years when Mother was talking to me about the Watson's, about the time, I think, when Mrs. Harry died, she said, "you know, I used to think, years and years ago, that Harry was in love with me. He was always in and out of the house, and later he was married from our house, and he was one of those who always called me Alice. (With women of my Mother's generation Christian names were seldom used. Generally, unless a friendship dated from school days, the married women were always addressed as "Mrs." ("Mrs. Side" or "Ma." Tom Bradley always called Mother, "Ma," and after him, all his children did and do.) "I knew he liked me, "she went on, "and I liked him. He made a good husband, too. He liked me a lot, I think. Do you know what? One day when the three of us were going up West together, your father got on the bus first, leaving Harry to help me on. Do you know what he said to me? 'Come along, dear!' Of course, it slipped out. He didn't mean anything. I thought it showed how he regarded me. Of course I didn't pay attention to it; acted as though I hadn't heard him. That's what he said, 'Come along, Dear'."

Mother's little romance. She must have treasured up that remark for nearly fifty years. I think she was always more than half in love with Harry Watson. Without knowing it. Anyhow, her Victorian prudery would have made her instinctively refuse to recognize such a disconcerting fact. As for me, I was probably in love with Will Watson, but in my innocence didn't know it. How old was I when he lived with us? Fourteen, fifteen? Not more. I knew I was fond of him of course. He was one of the "nice" uncles. All our parents' friends automatically became aunts and uncles to us children. He used to call me Rue, and tease me a little. I only remember one remark he ever made to me. "Don't make that moue at me," he said once, and I didn't know what he meant, and had to look up 'moue' in the dictionary. I suppose he began to treat me like a young lady, instead of a child, and I appreciated his attitude. I admired him immensely, and I was very sorry for him. Secretly, I yearned to comfort him, but hadn't the least notion how. He used to use swear words quite a lot. My parents didn't mind, that was just Will Watson, but when we girls were about they used to ssh-ssh-shush him and he always shut up. It was only a habit he had, but he would check himself before his friend's children. He never touched us, whereas Uncle Bradley would always fondle us.

So in my dream, I was looking at him with my old admiration, and yearning over him as I used to do, and thrilling all through with an excitement at his presence. All very erotic and neurotic of course, but that's the way it was. In slumber, I suppose, my body was calling for an appeasement it needed, and wouldn't get, so the old secret inner woman threw up this mirage of a lover to lull me a little. Well, well, it's a funny life.

Eve Curie states that though Marie did not have her children baptized and refused to teach them any religion, nevertheless their spiritual health was dear to her, and she tried "to preserve them from nostalgic reverie, from regret, from the excesses of sensibility." Evidently she didn't succeed in so protecting Eve. How can one be preserved from nostalgic reverie? I should like to know. It is a suffering I too would evade. But how? For, without warning, it envelops one like a fog fills the atmosphere, and more, even if one is clever enough to harness the waking thoughts, how defenseless one is in sleep. I try not to think of America, and busily I distract myself with this

Romford present, and what happens? In sleep I am back in America, back with my children, my friends, my youth, and I awake to this life, which is an endless purgatory. Only it isn't purging me from anything! I just endure, keeping my will set to a free future. If I can only live long enough. If I live?

I have finished the Curie book, and enjoyed every page of it. To read, her life was a great romance; but living it, she didn't find it one. In some of her pictures she reminds me of Miss Griffiths, a woman to whom I shall always pay homage. Miss Griffiths was always an inspiration, and even the memory of her can lift me up. In all Marie Curie's pictures there is a great sadness; whether the photograph shows her as an old or young woman, as a daughter, a wife, a widow, as a poor unknown student, or a world famous genius, she looks always the same, profoundly sad. My guess about her is that she never got over the loss of her religion. Her mother was a devout Catholic, and Marie was brought up as a good Catholic, with nothing but Polish Catholic tradition behind her. Then, in her student years, whilst still in Poland, she became a rationalist, a Positivist. That must have been the complete death of her soul, for she never recovered her religion. This is a very striking fact about her. To anyone, clever or stupid, it doesn't matter; to be born in Catholicism is to be irreducibly a Catholic. So, probably, she was always secretly longing to get back into her Catholicity, and never being able to return to it. I think that is why every portrait shows her so sad. The time was against her. It was an era of faith losing. Had she been born a little later, perhaps even if she had lived until now, she could have resumed her Catholicism, because now it is the fashion for the Intellectuals to go Catholic, and to defend their religion with their brains, as well as hold it in their emotions.

Poor Marie, she came in the between-times, and so was unlucky. This is only my guess, of course, but I think it is right. Apparently, she never gave up the use of the word 'soul' so she must have thought 'soul'. Well then, what are the connotations for a born and instructed Catholic? Every Catholic knows them, and I think that every Catholic who looks at these portraits of Marie Curie will see a woman who longed to return to her God and the practice of her religion, but who wasn't strong enough to do so. Poor Marie Curie!

EPISODE #10

- SUNDAY, MARCH 3, 1940 -

Artie came home for the weekend, which meant arriving at eight-thirty p.m. on Saturday night, and returning to the Barracks by eleven p.m. on Sunday, which meant leaving here at seven p.m.

Anyhow, we've seen him! He's very well.

- *MONDAY, MARCH 4, 1940* -

We received news from Harold. Kay gave birth to a nine and a half pound boy, January 17, 1940; baptized February 4th, 1940 as Robert Anthony. Mother and child are both doing well.

- *THURSDAY, MARCH 7, 1940* -

Auntie Mary died this morning. Dropsy. Gladys was called from Plymouth yesterday. We met at Mother's. Mother consented to allow Mary to be buried in the Brompton Cemetery grave, on top of Dad. The funeral will probably be on Tuesday next.

- TUESDAY, MARCH 12, 1940 -

I just got back from a trip to Boots, to change a book. It took me one hour. This is serious. I am very tired. Auntie Mary was buried yesterday, so I had another day in town, going first to the cemetery, and then on to Mother's. When I got back here I was quite exhausted. It is noticeable that I have lost considerable ground, physically. It must be because of this long shut-in winter we have just come through.

In the late fall I was quite pleased with myself. I was walking well and much easier, and better than for a long time past. Now, this past week or so, as the weather moderates, I find I am walking very badly again, and feeling great fatigue after doing so. This won't do, and I am determined to correct it. I will try to make it a habit to go out for a short walk every possible day. Of course I can't walk in the wet any more than I can walk on the snow or ice, but every day it doesn't rain I will try to go at least around the block. All last night I could hardly sleep for the ache in my limbs; for even my arms ached, from climbing in and out of buses, carrying bags, gas mask, etc. My legs ache today. I suppose they are the winter-long, unused muscles of the thigh, now called into action, rebelling. Anyhow, I am going to do something about it. I don't intend infirmities to increase on me if I can help it. These damned family legs are a curse all right, but I'm going to work at defying the curse.

So, though I only wanted to lie on the sofa, I made myself go out this afternoon. Every step was an effort, and it took me one whole hour to go and come, and now I'm just deadbeat. I went out, and I'll go out. I will walk.

- *WEDNESDAY, MARCH 13, 1940* -

It is the defeat of the Finns. An armistice has been arranged between the Russians and the Finns, and the Finns have to accept the Russian peace terms. This is a major disaster. Both Britain and France were standing by, ready to send men, but neither Sweden nor Norway would permit passage of troops through their country, so Finland is obliged to surrender and to cede to Russia more than Russia asked for before the war began. Oh this beautiful world!

- *THURSDAY, MARCH 14, 1940* -

I woke to find snow falling again, and it snowed until noon. Selma telephoned in midmorning and asked could she come to lunch. I had to say yes, though I did not want her. She came, and stayed until nine p.m., and now I am absolutely tired out. She is the most completely boring person it is possible to come across. The next time she tries to plant herself on me like this I shall find excuses.

- *FRIDAY, MARCH 15, 1940* -

At dinnertime Ted said he thought he would go and have an organ practice before coming in to tea, so I took the opportunity of a long afternoon to go to the movies. We haven't been to the pictures since New Year's, because of the bad weather and the blackout. So I went to the Ritz and saw Bette Davis and Miriam Hopkins playing in a version of an Edith Wharton story, *The Old Maid.*

After we had tea, Ted said, "I've a man coming to see me about something private at half-past seven. You might leave us alone, will you?"

I saw Ted let in a man in a very loud check overcoat and bright orange scarf. I thought it was someone about a house, or perhaps a 'knight', and left him to his men's talk. The fellow stayed a long time until nearly nine and then Ted came to fetch me into the parlor, very exhilarated. He didn't tell me the man's name, but he said, "That's a funny case for you! There's a man, born a Jew, but never brought up as one. In business in this town he heard me talking somewhere, knew I was a Catholic, telephoned to ask, could he come and have a talk with me, and wants to know whether I think he ought to become a Catholic. Nice, isn't it?"

"Very. Is his wife a Jewess?"

"No. Married to a Protestant. His wife turned Catholic some time ago and now he feels attracted to the church. Wonders what he ought to do about it. Got a son up at Cambridge. Good business. Gosh! The subjects we've been talking about!"

I didn't say anything more. What would be the use? I reconsidered the glimpse of the man I had caught in the hall; a smallish, elderly man, loudly dressed, and with a sheepish, apologetic smile on his face. Another romantic with an inferiority complex, I suppose. Having a talkfest with another little man about his thoughts and his soul. Grrr, it makes me sick. Only as recently as Wednesday night I had a dose of missionizing Catholicism.

Barbara Hayes called in, bringing some music for Ted, which she wants him to play at her wedding, which takes place on Easter Monday. Naturally we asked questions about the young man, and whether her family like him, and so on. She said, oh yes, they liked him, but the great drawback was that he was a

Protestant. Drawback. He was a good Protestant, so they had hopes of him, and if we all prayed hard enough, no doubt he would see the light, and come into the church. Wouldn't we please pray for her, and for her Jimmie's conversion?

Of course Ted effusively promised to do so with their monopoly of truth and righteousness! My God, how they weary me!

- SATURDAY, MARCH 16, 1940 -

Artie came in whilst I was washing up the tea things. He has leave until Sunday night.

- THURSDAY, MARCH 21, 1940 -

It is the official first day of spring. I have a sore throat; also a sore temper. Ted is being most aggravating and silly. He is 'playing' Holy Week to the limit, under-eating and over-praying, until he's unbearable. He is deliberately making himself miserable "for Christ's sake." I don't know what gratification or benefit Christ gets out of it, but I know what I get; which is a boring, scolding, unendurable fanatic. Throughout the week I have been listening to Ted talking at Artie, handing him out the most deadening platitudes and truisms with all the aplomb of a pope. As I listen to Ted, I just think he is one silly fool. He talks to Artie and me as though we knew nothing. Artie remains dutifully polite, and I say nothing.

Today I am cross. I think Ted is so preposterous. This is the incident that has enraged me. It occurred yesterday. As usual Ted got up early and went off to mass. The day went through as usual. Artie wasn't here in the afternoon. He had gone swimming with Pauline Dunball. At teatime Ted came in very late. The office closes at five. Tea is supposed to be about five fifteen p.m. Well, Ted didn't come until seven-twenty p.m. and then he didn't have his tea. "I've got to go to the church and see about the Easter music," he said, and went right out again, not returning until eight thirty; when he did eat his tea.

All right. That didn't annoy me. I am used to Ted's inconsiderateness about the tea meal. He treats the home like a restaurant and me like a servant, and comes when he is ready. At ten-thirty p.m. he went upstairs to bed. I decided to take a plate of cornflakes and hot milk before retiring. I have been sleeping very badly these last two weeks, and as I wanted to sleep, I thought the hot milk might induce sleep. Presently, after I had fixed the fire for the night, and was putting the scullery tidy and locking up, Ted appeared in the kitchen, in his pajamas, and in the devil of a temper. I looked at the clock. It was eleven ten p.m. So I had remained downstairs alone for forty minutes. Ted harangued me. He ordered me to bed. He asked me what I meant by "hanging about."

I said, "Don't talk to me like that."

He said, "I will. I'll talk to you just how I please. Go on upstairs, right away. I won't have you staying around like this."

I tried to laugh at him. He wouldn't have it. I said, "You went up early tonight. I thought you wanted to sleep."

"So I did," he said. "But you know I can't sleep until you settle down. You'll come to bed when I do or I'll sleep in another room. Do you hear me? Do you hear me?" And he stood behind me, threatening me, and herding me off like a sheep.

I was ready to go upstairs, so I went. I took my time about undressing, and I did not speak to him anymore, nor say goodnight when I got into bed. All the time I was undressing he kept raising his head from the pillow to look at the clock, and then dropping it back with a thud. He is so childish, so silly. I had trouble not to laugh. Well, I fell asleep.

This is Ted Thompson. This is my saint. He gets up very early every morning, so as to go to mass, because he wants to go. Then he wants to go to bed early, because he's tired, so I must be tired and go too. I'm not tired. Although the clock says ten-thirty, it's really only nine thirty because of 'summertime', which has already started, and my brain is not ready for sleep. I expect that is why I have been so wakeful these past few weeks. I must go to bed; that is his lordship's ruling. What about teatime? Doesn't he owe me the courtesy of coming to meals at mealtime? As Johnny says, "There ain't no justice."

Today I'm not exactly angry, nor depressed, either. I'm just weary; weary of enduring one fool man. I've no hatred against the fellow in my heart, but distaste and a dislike for his personality strikes deeper and deeper into my mind and sensibilities, distaste and a dislike, which is becoming permanent. I think he's one goddamn fool, and I long to get away from him, forever. I can't get away from him. We're married, God help us!

- THURSDAY, MARCH 28, 1940 -

Easter is safely past. Artie returned to barracks on Sunday evening. Cuth came home early this morning. He has leave until April Eighth.

I have been very ill with the flu but am on the mend now. I haven't been so ill for a very long time. On

Easter Sunday I was especially bad. I felt that even for me death wasn't very far away. However, I'm recovering. I am too sick to read; in these long days and nights of sleeplessness, my mind began its own composing again. It must be the spring! Anyhow, I'm all set to start out on the writing of a book. I can see the whole design of it, and get it down on the paper. I have already scribbled some notes for it, but I cannot begin to work at it systematically until after Cuthie goes back to Yorkshire.

I have an idea to recreate the large back bedroom as a sitting room, like it was when Charlie was here; and then I could work at my writing there, undisturbed. When I try to write in any of the downstairs rooms, I am always having to clear-away for meals, for visitors, etc. I was never able to work in the 'little room' that was too small for my comfort, but if I could dispose myself, as I wished, in that big back room, I think I could use that as a work room, and come and go up there, as domestic times suited. Perhaps I can persuade Cuthie to change the furniture around for me before he leaves us; but of course, if he doesn't want to, I can't shift it.

Today Carter Paterson brought me two chairs form Shepherds Bush. One is Auntie Daisy's rocker, and the other Auntie Mary Morris'. I am glad to get these chairs, but I don't know where I am going to place them. If I could re-make that room into a study, I could use them very nicely up there. Anyhow, I am very glad to receive them; they are nice chairs, and they belonged to dear aunts, and I shall use them somewhere or other.

Meanwhile, it is Cuthie's holidays. There is news this week of the birth of a son to John and Ruth, on March 6th. Kay and Harold had a second son born on January 17th. This child they have named Robert Anthony. Eddie and Chic are yet to be heard from. We know they are 'expecting' in March, and Cuth tells us their child was expected before Johnnie's.

- FRIDAY, APRIL 5, 1940 -

Edith and Monica were here for the day. My cold is still very bad. I have been sick again all this week.

I received important family news today. Ted and Cuthie have bought a pair of houses, numbers seventy-eight and eighty Western Road. They were auctioned on Wednesday, as one lot. Walter Wachett bid them in after they had passed Ted's set limit of seven hundred and fifty pounds. However, Ted especially wanted number seventy-eight for us, and offered Wachett a profit to split. This Wachett refused: he had bought them as one, and would only sell as one. The upshot is that Cuthie decided he could buy one and have it paid for by the time he comes out of the R.A.F. So, it has been so arranged. Ted introduced Cuth to the bank, opened an account for him at Lloyds, and two deeds are to be drawn up; one for Cuth on number eighty and one for us on seventy-eight. Number seventy-eight is vacant, and in eighty, Mr. and Mrs. John Thomson reside. (No connection of ours, just a coincidence.)

- SUNDAY, APRIL 7, 1940 -

Artie managed to get home for dinner. I told him the news about the Western Road houses. We celebrated with the last of the Christmas pudding and a little bottle of champagne that Cuthie had smuggled in from France.

- MONDAY, APRIL 8, 1940 -

Cuth left for Driffield soon after nine this morning. He says he'll probably be over the Rhine tomorrow.

- TUESDAY, APRIL 9, 1940 -

The war spreads. Germany invaded both Denmark and Norway this morning, at six o'clock. She announced to the world that she had taken these countries under her protection, to 'protect' them form the wicked Allies. Her protection works like this: she bombed Oslo from the air from two a.m. to five a.m. this morning. I suppose she 'protected' Poland.

- FRIDAY, APRIL 12, 1940 -

I went to the hairdresser's, to have my hair curled, the whole head. It should be done about June or July, but with the war intensifying and spreading as it is doing, I figured I better have a long session with the machine now whilst things are still quiet in Romford. I don't think many women are going to sit around in the beauty parlors once the bombs begin dropping.

- SUNDAY, APRIL 14, 1940 -

Edna Renacre came here for tea. She borrowed some more Balzac, and in addition I gave her six odd volumes of fiction, to keep. I suppose we must have at least a couple thousand books in this house, and the problem is how to move them? The answer is to dispose of as many as possible. Some we can give to the public library, some send away for the soldiers, and some we can give to our friends. There still will be hundreds we won't want to part with. This move is going to be similar to our move from Avenue A., Bayonne, to Bayside, Long Island. We are moving to a house, which is only half or less the size of this one. It's a good thing. I'll be glad to get rid of belongings.

EPISODE #11

- MONDAY, APRIL 15, 1940 -

I remain queer. In fact, I seem to have renewed my cold. Also, I'm walking very badly. I went downtown this afternoon, and hardly knew how to walk home.

Ted is very late for tea. He had been to the Western Roadhouse with Skilton to get ideas about the plumbing. Before he had finished eating, callers arrived. They were the John Thomson family from eighty Western Road. They stayed very late, but were agreeable company. In his youth, John Thomson had knocked around Canada and America, as a free-lance, much as Ted had done in the nineties, so they had a good time swapping stories.

- THURSDAY, APRIL 18, 1940 -

I am fifty-six today: in poor health, and poor sprits. I heard from Artie this morning, but no word from Cuthie. He is probably out bombing over Norway. I have not heard from him in over a week. English troops have been landed in Norway, but, so far, it seems to me, the Germans are winning; certainly they are holding their own, in most of Norway. The Allies have taken Karvik, and mutilated the German navy, but today's news says that the Germans are holding the iron-ore railways north of Karvik, and are fighting well.

As prophesized, the spring slaughter has begun. Artie is still with battalion in Sussex but for how long there now? No news from America. I received her usual sort of a letter from Mother.

The weather is abominable, very cold, very dull, and windy, and now commencing to rain. After a very severe winter, we are having a retarded spring. Frost every night this week. In Norway snow is still falling and, as in Finland, the troops are fighting on skis. What a war! What a world!

Well, this is the end of another seven-year period for me. For nearly a year I had been counting on it, looking forward to it, and thinking of it as another beginning; another fresh lap. In a way it will be, because of the purchase of the new house, the moving into of yet another home. This event was quite unforeseen by me. All through last fall I felt wonderfully well, and I imagined I was entering on a new period of fresh vigor, resilience, and good health. Apparently not; it was not to be. For weeks now I have been feeling wretchedly ill, and weak, and I have no zest left for anything. I am completely weary, in body, mind, and soul, and continuously I feel more ill than I remember feeling for years. Maybe I am only exhausted by the severity of the winter, and the strain of the war, but it is not like me to feel like this.

Well anyhow, it is still the end of one seven-year period, and the beginning of another. My life seems to fall into these natural periods more than most women. At twenty-one I married. During the next fourteen years I had my family, finishing with the twins when I was thirty-five. At forty-two came the end of Ted's business life. It was in 1926 that he resigned from office, and in 1927 he brought us back to England. In 1933, when I was forty-nine (seven times seven), I made my last trip to America, and it was then I made my wonderful, unforgettable round tour of the states. Now that I've reached fifty-six (eight sevens) I find that I have reached quiescence about the lots of mental troubles. All questions about belief, or beliefs, have left me. I am not concerned anymore about what I can or can't believe. This is a great gain and a great rest.

I have attained an inner peace, and I think it is a peace I shall never lose. I can recognize what doesn't matter, and never again will an argument ever coerce me. Circumstances may compel me to courses I shall not like, but they can never again compel my inner woman. She is free. What will she do with the next seven years? When I reach to sixty-three, if ever I do nine times seven, how will the world be, and how shall I be in it? Will my inner woman still be free and serene? Yes, I think she will be. What I have learnt, I have learnt; what I have reached into, I have reached into; and my joy no man can take from me. Absolutely, very literally, no man can take this from me. My husband may have become a bigger fool than ever, but my secret self he can never touch. I am myself, and I own myself, no matter what he thinks.

For now I know the things I know, and do the things I do, and if you do not like me so, to hell, my love, with you!

Of course I shall not be so outspoken as Dorothy Parker. Nevertheless, what Ted believes, or what he wishes to force me to believe, can never again have any effect upon me. I have outgrown him, passed him by.

So fifty-six is definitely some sort of an ending. What I am going into now, I do not know, but it is a new phase, I am sure. Perhaps destiny presents me the new house as a concrete symbol of it.

At tea tonight, speaking of the illness of young Clem Coppen's husband, a man of thirty only, with cancer, hence passing on to speak of Mother, and all her various operations, and her indomitable health and toughness, I remarked that Mother hadn't been able to pass her health and vitality to her children, not one of whom had ever been as strong as she was; to which Ted replied, "Of course not. That isn't surprising at all. Children naturally take after their fathers, and though your father was excitable enough, and vehement sometimes, he never had the energy and activity that your mother had. He was a slower tempo and less strong altogether. It is the father who stamps the children, always. It is the father who is the important one, always. That is why our Lord couldn't possibly have had a human father. It couldn't have been seemly. You couldn't imagine Saint Joseph being visited by a female angel, and begetting a child upon an angel, could you? Of course not! With the Blessed Virgin it was different. She could be overshadowed by the angel, the power of God, and not be contaminated by human intercourse. She received the seed from heaven, by the power of the Holy Ghost. It is simply unimaginable that our Lord could have had a human father! For then he would have been Joseph, not God, a sinful man."

This threw me into the abyss. I made no reply, not even the obvious one that the human embryo contains fifty-fifty of the hormones of its parents. I was simply stunned and disgusted by this fresh presentation of the old Christian and Jewish idea of the impurity of the flesh, the curse of sex, the virtue of Chastity, and the eternal inferiority of women. What is a wife? Still the old chattel: a concubine by night, and a servant by day; a creature without a soul; merely one of the creations of God, which exist for the use of man. My God! This Ted Thompson!

- SATURDAY, APRIL 27, 1940 -

Ted is at Arden Cottage. I have had a busy week, with visitors every day, so I am tired. Yesterday the legal business about the purchase of numbers seventy-eight and eighty Western Road was completed, and the keys handed over to us by the lawyers. Ted has been seeing Skilton about installing plumbing, stoves, etc., and Harvey, the builder, to get estimates about turning the house into flats.

The result for me is that I view our immediate future with acute apprehension of trouble. Ted is going to have to spend money, real cash, and that will hurt. He will niggle and haggle and make absurd economies, and just as absurd splurges, and every time he has to pay out he will be as disagreeable as hell. He will be on my tracks about household expenditure. He'll be after me turning out lights, fixing the stove, examining the pantry, and the dustbin; he'll hound me for a half pence, and he'll cry poverty, poverty until he'll rouse me to fury and I shall hate him with a singing hatred. I know Ted. I've had some of him before.

With it all, I shan't get what I want. He bought this property because he wanted to. He is going to fix it up the way he wants. Apparently he will consult me about items, but if I don't agree to what he has already decided, or if I should make suggestions contrary to his ideas, I shall be all wrong, and in great disfavor. I want to like this new house. I want to settle into it comfortably. I suspect it is going to be the last home Ted and I will ever have together, and it can be made very nice. Oh the job of it! We shall both of us lose our tempers over and over again.

I shall be disappointed about what I could get, and shan't, and Ted will grizzle about the spending indefinitely. Well there will be no peace in the Thompson family. I can see for some long time to come. What a life!

Cuthie is now stationed in the north of Scotland for quick access to Norway. He has also been over Denmark this week. The twenty-sevens were registering today. So far, the Germans are holding on in Norway, but their losses are heavy. Our navy has done well, and Sweden reports that around Oslo alone three thousand German dead have been washed ashore. War. This is more wisdom of men.

- *SUNDAY ARIL 28, 1940* -

I was in London during March, about the Aunties. I made inquiries at Stoneham's about the books of Annie C. Bill. They traced two of them for me, and sent them to me this week. I hadn't had time to look at them until today. I was examining one this morning whilst waiting for Ted to come into breakfast. (He left the house before seven a.m. and did not return until nine thirty, all this time for one mass and his private devotions.)

I was suddenly surprised at myself by falling into a panic. When I heard Ted's key in the door my heart began to beat like fury and I at once hid the book under the tea wagon. Why? It is a perfectly harmless book, and I have a perfect right to read it. Even if it was a rotten bad book, I've still got a perfect right to read it. You see what? I am afraid of Ted, still afraid of him! When we first married he began to deride the books I read, and this hurt me so much that I would never let him know what I was reading. I continued to read everything I wanted to read, but whatever the books were I would put them out of sight before he came home in the evenings; and on Sundays and holidays, when he was around the house, I never read anything at all except the newspapers and magazines. I never spoke to anyone, before him, of what I was reading. I kept up this habit until we left the states, and it is only since we have lived in Romford that I have read whatever books I wanted to, regardless of whether he was around or not. So this morning I was considerably surprised at myself, when in the midst of his approach I was flooded with feelings of guilt and fear.

Naturally my reason doesn't assent to any of this, but my natural, physical, animal woman did quake, was afraid. Still, as of old, she is afraid of this man.

It took me hours to quell my disquiet, and it was not until afternoon that my heart returned to its normal beat. Queer, isn't it? What one person can do to someone?

Evening. It is just as I foresaw: the economies are beginning at once. This afternoon Ted went round to Western Road to do some gardening at seventy-eight. He was very late returning for tea. It seems he had been visiting the other Thomson's in number eighty. Mr. Thomson showed him their upper floor. Now, number seventy-eight has no bathroom, so Ted has planned to create a bathroom in the back bedroom. This is a very long narrow room, and one-third of it could easily be walled off to make a small bathroom, but by doing this, a portion of the room would be left without light, so a window would need to be cut on the sidewall. Now Ted has taken this whole matter up with the Skilton's, and the room was to have been made into two, as I have just outlined.

In number eighty, where a bath and basin has been installed, everything has been left exposed; Ted has decided to do without a partition and a window in our house, because that will be cheaper. Exactly. It is cheap and nasty. He will discover other and similar economies. Probably he will dispense with a carpenter altogether, and all the built-in fixtures we need will be put up by his own butchering. This is quite likely. The furniture he said could be recovered will not go to the upholsterers. I never answered him when he told me of this cheaper bathroom plan. What could I have said? If he won't spend money, I shall have to make do, as per usual.

I first saw through this new house on the evening of Saturday April 13. Ted took me round there on his way to Bert's, and left me to see through it alone. It was about half past seven in the evening, between lights. The effect of the place on me was to depress me. When I got back here, I began to cry and I think I cried all night. When Ted got back from Bert's, I was hysterical. I told him I couldn't make the move; I couldn't live there. Wisely, he refrained from discussing the matter with me then but he assured me later in the week that he did intend to modernize the place, to install proper plumbing and stoves, etc. Then when I saw it the second time, going round there with him Sunday a week ago, the twenty-first, on a bright sunny afternoon, the place did look more attractive, did show possibilities for being made into a comfortable habitation. I felt reassured then. Now, home he comes with ideas as to how he needn't do what he had planned to do, Gosh! It's the devil!

- *MONDAY, APRIL 29, 1940* -

I had a nice visit from Ethel Coppen today, but disagreeable words with Ted this evening. He began badgering me about the removal of our books. So far I haven't been able to do any sorting out at all. I had visitors every day last week and this week is beginning the same. This is a job that needs thinking about and I must be in the mood for the thinking, or I can't do it at all. Ted wants to drive me to it at once. When? How soon? When will I know? And so on. When I told him I didn't know when I could do it, he became insulting, said I was a fool, wouldn't cooperate, and I was more mulish than Selma. When I protested, "Don't talk to me like that!" he said he would talk to me just as he pleased, that I was a fool, and that he thought less of my sense than ever. I said that when he talked to me like that he was being deliberately spiteful, and that it would do no good, because such talk only antagonized me. He said, then I was a bigger fool even than he had thought, and he went off by himself to the dining room. There he is now, listening to Shakespeare on the wireless. What a petty fellow! When he speaks to me so contemptuously, it is the inner man speaking, and I can see that is how really contemptuously he thinks of me. That doesn't help at all.

I often think Ted is a fool, but I am very careful never to tell him so or even give him an inkling to guess on. I dissemble my thoughts. I play up to him all I can. It is my undeviating policy to live at peace, for I saw enough of marital quarrels between my parents, and I don't want any quarreling in my life. Just the same, I have an awful crushed feeling tonight.

- *TUESDAY, APRIL 30, 1940* -

I have been putting away all my papers. I simply cannot write. So now I've lost stroke again. Maybe when the moving is over and we are seated in the new house, maybe I can begin again. For me, to write a continuous work without steady hours of reliable leisure is impossible.

Ted is still disagreeable. So far today he has not spoken to me yet. Of course he was out to early mass this morning, just the same.

- *FRIDAY, MAY 3, 1940* -

This is our 35th wedding anniversary. I thought perhaps we might have celebrated it a little; but no, Ted remains disagreeable and aloof. I don't think he has spoken to me once today. Well, this is the end of another seven-year period. What will the next seven-year period of our marriage be like? Shall we grow less critical and kinder? I wonder.

EPISODE #12

- SATURDAY, MAY 4, 1940 -

I was awakened during the night by the airplanes, which were screaming about quite a lot. This is not a bit unusual nowadays. One day this week a German bomber crashed at Claxton, causing one hundred and fifty-six casualties and destroying two streets. This was not deliberate bombing but an accident. It had been mine laying, so carried much explosives. Well, even here, I heard what must have been the detonations. Ted doesn't hear these night noises, but is able to sleep right through them. By the way, our forces have evacuated themselves from Norway during this week, a very disturbing setback for us. So far, it seems to me Hitler wins everywhere he strikes; and as for Mr. Chamberlain and Winston Churchill, public opinion begins to be that they are too complacent and then too late. This isn't a war record.

Joan arrived this morning. She has come for the weekend. George returned to France April 16th, and Joan is staying in Hammersmith with Mother for the present.

- SUNDAY, MAY 5, 1940 -

Joan remarked that she had been going up to Westminster Cathedral, intended to visit the Brompton Oratory soon, and asked, would I take her to church with me today? Well, I said I would, so we got ready and I took her to High Mass at St. Mary's at Hornchurch.

When I was explaining the missal to her, I noticed that I had marked the collect for this day in the missal. It is: "Almighty, Everlasting God, grant that our will may be ever devoted to thee, and that we may serve thy majesty with a sincere heart. Through our Lord."

All this is something strangely coincidental. For I have been thinking of late whether perhaps I might resume attending mass again. Noting all these various finales which seem to occur now, with the beginnings of the new periods, and the taking up of residence in a new house, and all the events occurring about now, the time especially associated with the Holy Ghost, that member of the Holy Trinity which is so especially appealing to my crank mind. I had thought that perhaps I would resume the practice of my religion right now at this Whitsuntide. Then along comes Joan, who asks me to take her to church today. So we went. It was good, easy, peaceful, consoling.

Although Joan had no idea how to follow the mass, yet she was pervious to the atmosphere of serenity and devotion. As for myself, I entered into peace; it was as though I had never missed mass at all.

- MONDAY, MAY 6, 1940 -

Joan returned to Hammersmith before dark. It has been a good visit. News from Cuthie, he is back at Driffield. He writes, "Scotland is a pain in the neck."

I am very sleepy. I think it is the Spring Day. Anyhow, I'm tired from so much talking with Joan. I only see her about once a year, so we talk like a house afire.

Ted is still very disagreeable, and I expect he will remain so, until he has paid his last bill. He was very sarcastic at lunch about me not writing to Dorothy. Last week he climbed up into the attic, to find out what was there, and found two large trunks; one of ours, one of Dorothy's. He said if I ever wrote to Dorothy, I could tell her to have it fetched away. I replied, I never wrote to her, and I didn't know her address anyhow. At lunch today, he asked me had I written to Dorothy. I replied, of course not. Why? I asked did he wish me to write to her? Then he was off! Ten unending minutes of biting sarcasm about my indifference, etc., ending with, "Well, will you write to Dorothy?" I reply as, "No." It's his affair as much as mine. If he wants her to take her trunk away at once, why can't he write to her about it? Why am I a sinner because it hadn't occurred to me to do so?

O, funny man! He does make me tired. Another thing that makes me tired are these midday meals. Three square meals a day, and Ted at every one of them. We see too much of each other. A woman needs her day to herself. Midday dinner is a nuisance. That is what we have had ever since we returned to England. It means we are never free of each other for more than four hours at a stretch, often only three hours. Contact is too unbroken. No wonder there's so much friction between us. We need rest from each other, and space between meetings. I need rest and spacing from the household chores. Even if I could have only one long day a week to myself it would be a blessed relief. But no, domestic life hasn't been arranged that way. Life in England is a treadmill.

Men are fools. This fact has been noticed before, ten thousand times ten thousand; but I will note it again; men are fools. Why is the general war going on? It is because men will have it. Men are fools, collectively and individually. Men are fools. In the night, Ted loved me. Why couldn't he have loved me before? Now for both of us our nerves are assuaged, the tension between us is lessened; and it is all so simple! Physical contact in affection. Lord! What fools we mortals are!

- *FRIDAY, MAY 10, 1940* -

Germany has invaded Holland and Belgium, and completely over-runs Luxembourg. The news came through soon after six this morning. They have landed troops at the ports, and men from the air by parachute. The attack from the air has been terrific also. Both Holland and Belgium have appealed to us for help, and we are going to their assistance instantly. Half an hour ago our government, through the BBC, broadcast to all our Civil Defense Forces to stand-by and to be ready for any emergency; and to civilians to resume continuous carrying of gas masks, the putting of all home defense precautions in order, and for everybody to immediately acquaint themselves with their nearest air-raid shelter. Attack on England is imminent. The Germans may begin bombing us now, at any moment.

Perhaps the Germans have been encouraged to this move by the Rebate in Parliament this week on the Norwegian operations, the Division in the House, the criticisms of Mr. Chamberlain, and the Cabinet crisis. Who knows? Anyhow, here's the war, in hellish earnest. Ten p.m. Mr. Chamberlain has resigned, and the King has appointed Winston Churchill as Prime Minister. So, another cabinet shuffles.

- *SATURDAY, MAY 11, 1940* -

A special order has been passed to eliminate the Whitsuntide holiday. Monday will be a business day. All special Whitsun sport events have been cancelled, all rail and road excursion traffic, and all factories, banks, stock exchange, government offices, etc. will carry on as usual.

- *SUNDAY, MAY 12, 1940* -

Whit Sunday

It is a gloriously beautiful day. Its blueness and sunshine is like the September weather when the war started.

Reports from the Netherlands are most serious. The Germans are landing parachutists by the hundreds. These Germans are disguised. Some even wear Dutch uniforms. Some are disguised as priests and even nuns. They are very young men, and many are dressed as women. When caught, they are "wiped out" the report says. As usual the Germans are bombing everything in sight, and especially the refugees along the roads. For pure wanton destructiveness they are even machine gunning the cattle in the fields. I went again to St. Mary's for High Mass this morning and was able to pray.

Princess Juliana and her two babies, and Prince Bernhard, arrived in London this morning; and late this afternoon Queen Wilhelmina arrived also. She had been brought here on a British warship. Both the King and Queen met her at Liverpool St., as well as her own children, and she has accepted the hospitality of the King at Buckingham Palace. She had to flee for her life. The Germans meant to abduct her. In Norway, too, they tried especially hard to capture King Haakon. The fighting in Holland and Belgium is simply terrific.

- WEDNESDAY, MAY 15, 1940 -

At seven a.m. we heard that the Dutch have laid down their arms. After the Germans re-captured Rotterdam yesterday, the Netherlands Commander-in Chief issued an order to his troops concerned to cease fighting. To continue resistance was hopeless.

Now the struggle for Belgium proceeds. Already the battlefront extends over one hundred miles, from the Albert Canal to Llugwy, where the Germans are expected to try to break through the Maginot Line. There is furious fighting at Sedan, and a very great battle is expected in front of Brussels.

- SUNDAY, MAY 19, 1940 -

Trinity Sunday

I made an effort, and it was an effort, both physically, and of the will, and went to St. Edward's for High Mass at eleven. Now I have resumed, I will continue. Coming out of church, joined by Mrs. Jude and Mary Bernadette, and Mrs. James. When we got to the Laurie, I was very pleased to see Ted waiting for me at the entrance to Ives Gardens. Here a Mr. Simpson, who appropriated Ted and walked ahead with him, joined us!

However, I was deeply pleased Ted had come to meet me, all the same; and I pray to God there is a new beginning for we two together, to be added to my other beginnings.

- *TUESDAY, MAY 21, 1940* -

We received three letters from Cuthie this morning. Two for me and one for Ted all posted from Driffield. So he is safe, so far, thank God. The battle now raging in France and Belgium is the greatest of all time. It goes on without ceasing, day and night.

General Petain, now eighty-four years old, has been recalled from Madrid, where he had been sent as Ambassador at the end of the Spanish Civil War, and made Deputy Prime Minister of France. General Weygand, now seventy-three, has been recalled from Syria and appointed Chief of Staff of National Defense (in place of General Gamelan). It was these two great soldiers, under Foch, who finally brought victory to the Allies in the Great War, twenty years ago.

Every day for a week Dutch and Belgian refugees have been pouring into our southern ports, and, as in 1914, we are going to take care of them for the duration of the war. They have nothing left them but their lives. Many of them are wounded and are brought ashore in stretchers. Some infants have been born whilst their mothers were in the boats. The Germans deliberately machine-gun the refugees as they walk along the roads. War! German War!

- WEDNESDAY, MAY 22, 1940

Last night at seven p.m. we received a telegram from the air ministry to say that our son, Sergeant 581052, squadron seventy-seven, was reported missing. A letter would follow. The nine o'clock broadcast news reported that during the night a large force of R.A.F. bombers attacked troop concentrations in Cambrai Le Cateau St. Quentin area and that from these operations five of our aircraft failed to return. So we suppose Cuth were in one of these five.

The battle is frightful. The Germans have taken Amas and Amiens, and have reached as far as Abbeville in their drive to the coast. God help us all!

When Ted went out last night to church for benediction, for the May devotions, he showed the telegram to Father Bishop. About nine o'clock Father Bishop telephoned us that he would offer this morning's mass for Cuthie and for our intentions. This was kind. I could not go out to Mass but I pray just the same. Today work has gone on as usual; Mrs. Bull here cleaning, Miss Coppen calling. Poor Cuthie, poor Cuthie!

- THURSDAY, MAY 23, 1940 -

The letter from the Air Ministry arrived by the first post this morning. They tell us that Cuthie was with the squadron that was sent out bombing in the vicinity of Amiens, in the morning of May 21st, but that his machine failed to return to its base, so he must be counted missing. They add that this does not necessarily mean that he is either killed or wounded, and that if and when they receive extra knowledge of him, they will report to us at once. Yes, there is a hope he may still be alive. Sometimes crews escape from destroyed machines. He may be a prisoner behind the lines. He may be lying in a German hospital, or he may be with God in heaven. Wherever he is, we will pray for him without ceasing. The terror is surely upon England now. On Sunday ten thousand more children were evacuated from Kent and Essex; they were sent to Wales.

On Tuesday night we had raids over this neighborhood. The guns began about one thirty. Neither Ted nor I were asleep. We had gone to bed grieving for Cuthie, and were wakeful. At two ten a.m. there was a most terrific explosion, which we supposed was a bomb. We did not get up, because no warning was sounded, so we inferred the action was not immediately over Romford. The firing went on for some time, thud-thud, and airplanes seemed to be screaming about everywhere. Then everything died down. Soon after four o'clock the racket began again, though there was no great explosion as at two. Last night was quiet, or else we were so tired that we slept through everything.

The weather is beautiful. This morning's times say the British have counter-attacked between Anas and Donai, but the results are not known and the French morning communiqué reports the re-taking of Arras.

- *SATURDAY, MAY 25, 1940* -

Agnes Brauncy brought her fiancé here this afternoon to look at our Jacobean dining room suite, and they bought it outright. I had intended to go to confession today, but these visitors prevented me. This evening, utterly exhausted, I cannot possibly go out.

- *SUNDAY, MAY 26, 1940* -

A day of public prayer, asked for by the King, and observed by every sect and denomination. I went out to early mass with Ted, at St. Edwards, but could not go up for communion. The church was packed and practically everybody going up to the rail, as at Christmas or Easter. When we returned home, Ted told me that he had asked Father Bishop to say tomorrow's mass for Cuthie. So I asked Ted to telephone Father Bishop for me, and ask him would he hear my confession today. He set the time for four forty-five p.m. It had been my intention to ask him tomorrow to hear me, so that I might take communion on Tuesday for Cuth. Father Bishop is very kind and very understanding.

- *TUESDAY, MAY 28, 1940* -

I went again to communion this morning with Ted. It is a week today since Cuth was lost. At eleven o'clock this morning came news that King Leopold of the Belgians had ordered the army under his command to cease fighting. This is most shocking news. M. Reynaud, the French Premier, gave the news in a broadcast. He told Paris, and the world, that the Belgium Army, on the order of King Leopold, who acted against the advice of his responsible ministers, has surrendered. Since four o'clock this morning the French and the British armies have been fighting alone in the north against the enemy. They still hold Calais, but the B.S.F. have had to evacuate from Boulogne.

However, at noon today, Mr. Pierlot, the Belgian Premier, broadcast from Paris, repudiating King Leopold, calling him a traitor, and accusing him of breaking the Belgian Constitution and saying that the Belgian Government intend to form a new army and to fight on. The battling is terrific. God help the world!

- THURSDAY, MAY 30, 1940 -

This is my last writing in this house. We move into number seventy-eight Western Road tomorrow. I am now about to bury this volume in my hatbox, so au-revoir. God help us and keep us all. Amen.

EPISODE #13

- TUESDAY, JUNE 11, 1940 -

Seventy-Eight Western Road, Romford

This is my first writing in the new home, and it is a writing of doom. Not my doom, but Europe's. Yesterday, at six p.m. Mussolini announced from Rome that Italy was at war with Great Britain and France. This is a stab in the back, and was stigmatized as such last night by President Roosevelt, broadcasting from Virginia. The terrific battle of Somme-Aisne has been going on ceaselessly for seven days and nights; the Germans smash in and the Allies keep retreating, and it is at this moment, when France is staggering under the Germans, that Mussolini, without reason or provocation, decides to enter the war, fighting for Hitler. King Leopold played the Judas two weeks ago, now it is Mussolini's turn to act the part. What will be the next tragedy?

What I specifically want to note today is the weather. We have enjoyed one of the most beautiful springs and early summers that England has ever known. There is light, color, sunshine and warmth everywhere. The flowers and the foliage have been perfect, more beautiful than ever before. Last Saturday and Sunday we were very hot, but the blueness and goldenness remained unabated.

Yesterday, Monday the 10th, something extraordinary happened to the weather. I rose early to go to mass with Ted (the mass this Monday and Tuesday was offered for Cuthie). It was a dull morning yesterday, when we left the house at seven a.m., but when we came out of church at eight a.m. an awful blackness filled the sky. It looked as though a frightful storm was imminent. Nothing happened; no rain, no wind, no thunder or lightning, only a spreading blackness and an awful oppressiveness of the atmosphere. This state continued all day. It was dark like a black winter's day, and we had to switch the lights on to work by. It was an uncanny day. Then at six o'clock came the news that Mussolini was at that moment announcing to the world the entry of Italy into war against the Allies. I thought of the narrative of the crucifixion: "and darkness covered the earth." The very heavens protested against Mussolini's callousness and treachery.

In myself, I am at peace; a peace I have not known for years. I am full of grief, too, grief for Cuthie, grief for the world. I am full of apprehension, too. Where is Artie? We have not heard from him since June third. The probabilities are he is in France.

Yesterday Churchill announced that further troops had been safely landed in France, and that more were ready to cross over. The crucial battle of France is being fought now, and England will send quickly all the help she probably can. So if Artie isn't in France already, I expect he soon will be. God keep him. Deliver us from evil. Amen.

I pray all the time. For Cuth, for Artie, and for all the young men who are fighting to defend our freedom and civilization. That is why I am at peace. Deep and deep as is my grief, deeper yet is my peace, because at long last I have made my peace with God. This is the true peace, and there is nothing else in all of life like it. Whatever happens to us, to our lives, to our children, I pray God to keep me, and all of us, in His Grace, now, and forever more. Amen.

- *FRIDAY, JUNE 14, 1940* -

Today the Germans have entered Paris. Hitler swore to take it on June 15th. So he is one day ahead of schedule.

Last night, Thursday, M. Reynaud broadcast an appeal to Roosevelt and America, begging for speedy help. Roosevelt has cabled back that the American government would redouble their efforts to send airplanes and munitions, as long as the allied governments continue to resist.

- *SUNDAY, JUNE 16, 1940* -

At eleven thirty p.m. the French wireless announced that the Reynaud Cabinet had resigned. Marshal Petain had been asked to form a new cabinet, in which General Weygand would be Vice President of the Council. The cabinet had met three times today while M. Reynaud was on his way to the last meeting, at ten p.m. A heavy German bomber bombed a small village square where his staff was waiting, killing thirty-eight people, including eight soldiers, and wounding sixty. What shall we hear tomorrow?

- *MONDAY, JUNE 17, 1940* -

One p.m. there is news, not yet confirmed, that Marshall Petain, has sent a message to Hitler, asking for an armistice, and the discussion of terms of peace. There was an agreement between England and France that neither should seek peace separable, so now what?

The war is awful beyond words. Germany is winning all the way. No country can stand up to her. Her men and munitions are unending. France is beaten. The Germans have yet beaten her once again.

Then what about us? Will the English continue to fight? If in France, Germany can beat the combined armies of France and Britain, what could England do against her alone? The dead; they have died in vain.

- SATURDAY, JUNE 22, 1940 -

Hitler received the French delegation yesterday and informed them of his terms for an armistice. He chose as the scene of the ceremony the railway carriage in the forest of Compiegne, where Marshal Foch granted the Germans an armistice on November 11, 1918. The terms offered have not yet been published, but their objects are described as:

To prevent a resumption of hostilities

To provide all necessary safeguards to Germany for the continuation of the war against Britain

To create the necessary conditions for a new peace based on "reparation of the injustice committed by force against the Reich."

So what? The French Cabinet has been sitting most of today, and no armistice has been signed up 'til now, eight fifteen p.m. Winston Churchill broadcast on Tuesday night, saying we would fight on "'til the curse of Hitler is lifted from the brows of men."

Tuesday night the Germans raided us, sending over at least one hundred bombers. A row of houses was demolished in a Cambridge town, causing a loss of fourteen lives. Other damage was done, in Suffolk and Essex. They were very near to us here, and we had a very noisy night indeed. Just the same we stayed in bed. Much damage was done at Southend, and at WestCliff the new technical school was demolished.

Wednesday night again they raided us; they sent more machines but did less damage. Now we can expect bombing nightly until the end. It is very frightening, but after a while one feels it's ignoble to show fear, and then ceases to worry. What will be, will be? One simply takes the reasonable precautions, and prays.

Ted has taken the week off from Wednesday. We have been fixing the blackouts, laying linoleum, etc. Today Stone's carpet man was here, cutting and binding our carpets to fit those smaller rooms. The carpenter started his odd job yesterday, so gradually we are progressing towards comfort.

It is now a month since Cuthie was lost. His name is in the Roll of Honor in today's *Times*.

George Godfrey too is missing. Joan wrote me on Tuesday that she had received a letter from the war office, notifying her George was posted as 'missing', date unknown. Poor Joan.

- *TUESDAY, JUNE 25, 1940* -

The German war against France finished at twelve thirty a.m. this morning. At one a.m. the Germans started raiding us in earnest. The warning was given at one a.m., and here in Romford the all clear was not sounded until four a.m. The warning was given practically all over England. The German machines were coming over in wave after wave. Ted and I went downstairs, and stayed there 'til the all clear was given. We sat in the dark in the dining room, listening for the guns and saying our prayers.

Eight p.m. Ted at Arden Cottage and I am sitting here in the window of my new bedroom. I am well, but have a bad leg. I have an open wound on my left ankle nearly as large as the palm of my hand, and very painful. I suppose this has been brought about by the work of the moving and the heat. Anyhow, I haven't had an open leg for years. It won't get better, of course, until I go to bed and stay there until it heals. At present this is out of the question, for there are still all sorts of workmen to wait about for electricians, gas fitters, the carpenter, and the painter.

The finishing of this house goes very slowly. Men come and do a bit and then stay away for days. The carpenter never came at all this week, though I was looking for him daily. So with the others, but if I do go out somebody is sure to come. I missed the electrician by going out, and also the carpet fitter. However, someday the last workman will say goodbye and then I can take to my bed until cured.

I have been having vacuum cleaner salesman around too. After trying out three different machines, I decided on a "Hot-Point" and then had to persuade Ted to buy it for me. I am happy to say he did buy it, and I am really very glad of that. In this house we are living more on carpets than linoleum. And a vacuum cleaner is really essential for comfortable clean housekeeping.

Also I have been writing letters. The Germans are raiding us daily and nightly now, and most of the casualties are civilians. We have not had a warning in Romford, though the area is flown over every night by solitary bombers since the one of June 24th, 25th…but I made up my mind on that night to write a good letter to every one of the boys whilst I knew I was still in the land of the living. I finished my last letter to Johnnie on the 4th.

That day we received the news of the destruction of the French Fleet at Oram and the taking over of the French warships at Alexandria, and all in the British ports. This is another tragedy of the war, but it was absolutely essential that the French vessels should not fall into German or Italian hands to be used against us. The Petain government has already become the abject tool of the Nazi's and speaks only as Hitler allows it to speak.

The collapse of France is complete. This week has been alluded to as Invasion week, because Hitler promised to invade us this week, and overthrow us. However, he hasn't arrived yet! Possibly his plans have been disarranged by troubles in the Balkans. Romania is breaking up now. Russia put in an ultimatum to Romania last week, demanding the cession to her of Bessarabia and Boulhovina and before the answer could be given just walked in. Romania appealed to Germany and foreswore her Anglo-French treaty, but Hitler did nothing for her anyhow. Italy is getting a pasting. She doesn't have to fight in France, because of the armistice, but she's got to fight Britain, and now she is getting the worst of it in Africa. Marshal Balbao is dead, killed in a plane crash. Well, Italy is not fighting black Abyssinians now.

- *SUNDAY, JULY 7, 1940* -

It is a very muggy day, with very heavy rain and hail. After the storm the sky cleared to cloudless blue, and then the guns began. They were not in this immediate vicinity. Probably they were at Dagenham, or over the river. Anyhow, from about half past two 'til after five o'clock we heard the A-A guns continuously. This made us restless. To settle us Ted went down to the garden and picked a lot of raspberries and currants, and I set to and made a batch of pastries. So we ate hot raspberry pie for tea. The evening was quiet.

- MONDAY, JULY 8, 1940 -

I am feeling considerably exasperated. Lord Woolton, the Minister for Food, has just been broadcasting. He has suddenly clamped on us further rationing. This concerns margarine and cooking fats, restaurant meals, and tea. Until now tea has not been rationed, but now, without any warning, we are informed that starting from tomorrow the allowance of tea will be set at two ounces per week per person. Considering what very heavy tea drinkers the English are, this is a very drastic ruling. However, it isn't that, that makes me feel so cross; it is the whole speech of the man, and the very tone of his voice. There was something so cajoling and so condescending in his phrasing, and something so unctuous and oily in his tone, I suddenly felt I hated him, and everything he stands for. Here again is a rich man instructing the poor how to be happy in their poverty, content under restrictions. Does anyone suppose his pantry isn't full of chests of tea? Does anyone think he is going to restrict his consumption of tea to two ounces per week? Of course not!

Yes, I feel cross. Cross with the war, and the stupidity of men who wage war. War is the greatest folly of mankind. There is a constant stream of propaganda, which pours over us from the radio. Speeches, speeches, speeches; heroics and heroics, and for what? They want us to make war, to fight war, to endure it and to pay for it. It makes me sick listening to the orators. I feel I'm not going to deny myself voluntarily for the war. I'll endure what I have to because I can't help myself, but I'm not going to penalize myself where the authorities can't compel me to. I've lost a son already in the damned war. The smarmy talk of oratorio's about self-sacrifice leaves me cold. Let the politicians do some self-sacrificing. Then I might listen to them with agreement more readily. The damn fool politicians, men, old men, make a war to suit themselves; they make the young men fight it and they invite the women to pay for it. Well, they will solicit me in vain. I say, damn the war. Let the war makers get on with it. I'll not help them.

- *WEDNESDAY, JULY 10, 1940* -

Eleven a.m. and I am still alive. I thought the end was upon us last night. Just after the nine o'clock news began, whilst the announcer was telling us of the putting out of action of the French battleship Richelieu, air-battle began, practically immediately over-head. The noise was incessant. But the machines were so high we couldn't see them. We have heard them tearing about all right! We closed the windows and pulled the curtains, and sat still, expecting any minute to be bombed or set on fire. However, nothing hit us, and after about an hour everything quieted down again.

Ted opened a bottle of his precious port, and we each had a drink at bedtime. I was afraid to go to bed; afraid the raiding would begin again. It didn't. So here we are in the morning, still intact. I feel sick. I feel as though my insides have been torn out. What will happen to us as the moon comes to the full, God knows?

EPISODE #14

- *MONDAY, JULY 15, 1940* -

At five fifty p.m. we received a telegram from Ruislip, saying: “Inform you your son Sgt. Thompson; R.A.F. is a prisoner of war. Letter follows.”

Thank God!

- *WEDNESDAY, JULY 17, 1940* -

Letter confirming news about Cuthie received today. No details. Simply says that they have been informed through the Red Cross at Geneva, that he is a prisoner, at Dulag Luft.

Also, several sheets of type received from the Red Cross, telling how to get in touch with prisoners, etc. This is Ted’s birthday, so the good news is the best gift in the world for him. To celebrate we went to the movies tonight. It is our first jaunt in months.

- *FRIDAY, JULY 19, 1940* -

I called the doctor this evening to look at my leg, which has begun watering. It has been getting worse and worse lately, but today got to where it is unendurable. I called Dr. Keighly, as she is only a few doors away. I was frightened, and wanted a doctor quickly. She said I ought to be in bed. Of course, I know that but bed is impossible at this time, with workmen coming and going, and all this long drawn out mess of the move still around me. It seems to me this place will never get straightened out, but I suppose it will, someday.

- *MONDAY, JULY 22, 1940* -

Dr. Keighley in this evening. She has drawn up a diet sheet for me. She declares she can reduce my weight, and without drugs, if only I will follow her instructions. Well, I'll follow them all right. If I could lose weight it would certainly be a darned good thing. My leg is still weeping, though not so profusely.

- *WEDNESDAY, JULY 24, 1940* -

Mother came to see me today. She looks remarkably well, very stylish and handsome. She had on a dark blue wool-crepe suit, and blue hat in the latest style. She looked very elegant.

We have had a continuous stream of callers since the news of Cuthie came out. I did not know he had so many friends; so many people who are deeply glad to hear of his safety. Yes, thank God, thank God, Cuthie is safe! Thank God.

- *MONDAY, JULY 29, 1940* -

I have been reading a book over the weekend, which pleased me, much: *Let the Band Play Dixie,* by Ursula

Branston. It is an account of an English girl's trip, by autobus, through the southern states of America. She had a job with the BBC but she resigned it, because of her longing, after reading a life of Stonewall Jackson, to see all the southern states. She landed in Baltimore, in June 1938, and she stayed in America until the September crisis at Munich, when her own patriotism hurried her back to London in October. This girl appreciates America, and although her book doesn't make me homesick because I know a return to America is at present as impossible as a trip to the moon, still, it makes me realize how essentially and fundamentally I am American. The tangible result was to make me sit down today and send in an order to Bumpus for half a dozen American books in their latest catalogue. Chief among these is a first edition second volume, *History of the Rise of American Civilization*, by the Beards. I hope I get it. This was a new book when I was in New York in 1933. I didn't see it then, not since. It was published in England so didn't reach the libraries.

I ordered a few others, about America, or by Americans. I haven't bought any books for a long time, and when we had to make a grand clearance for our move, and give away literally hundreds, I said I wouldn't ever buy any more books. There you are; I'm an addict! Anyhow, what I figure is this; and not only about books, but about all other desirable things: better get them whilst we can, and whilst we know we are still alive to enjoy them. We might be dead tomorrow. We might be dead today. Every day the German bombs are taking toll of British lives; life for everybody in these islands is dreadfully precarious. Last Friday night this neighborhood was bombed again. Bombs fell and we heard them falling in Worley, Dagenham, and Laughton. In Laughton they destroyed two houses and killed people; in Dagenham they destroyed thirty houses, and killed one woman and three children; in Worley they fell in an open space, but killed a fireman who was entering a shelter. So they are just as likely to fall in Western Road, or South Street, or Park End Road, or anywhere.

There is now seldom a warning. Messerschmidt's fly six miles high, and drop their bombs at random. So, as we're only young once, only live once—I think we feel, I know I do—let us make sure of today, whilst we know we have it. All the exhortations on the radio to save leave me cold. Save for what? Annihilation? The politicians decreed the war; let them pay for it. They tax us excessively, anyhow, and ration us without warrant. Why should they consume our savings and our pleasure money too? I don't see it. So, since death has camped on the doorstep, I intend to suck every drop out of my orange, before he crosses the threshold and grabs my rind. I'll buy books, clothes, anything I really want and have the price for. Tomorrow can take care of itself. The chances are that tomorrow I may not be alive to do anything about it. Nevertheless, I hold onto my inner determination to live to be one hundred if I can. I pray and pray. I pray at night until I fall asleep. I pray every time I wake in the night, and I pray every morning after a night in bed, to find one is still alive in this world. I say, thank God for another day. I will live if I can. The Germans may kill me but I won't allow them to depress my soul. The British government may ration us drastically but I don't intend to ration myself on any of the things I care for, so long as they are in the market, and I have the price to pay for them.

I loathe people who talk about self-sacrifice. We are all sacrificed, willy-nilly. All our young men turned into soldiers, for what? There is death and destruction everywhere, and everywhere the will to death. It's crazy. I have a will to life, and with help of God, I will live, I won't be miserable. I'll live happily. I've made our lives as pleasant as possible, with all the means at my disposal. I will have books and music and flowers and good clothes and good food. I believe in God, and I praise him. I place my dear ones, in God's hands now and myself, so do I place our futures in his hands too, in this world and the next. God will take care of tomorrow. I'm not going to worry about it.

- *SATURDAY, AUGUST 3, 1940* -

The word for today is forlorn. When Dr. Keighley came in to see me on Monday, she ordered me to bed and I have been there until today. Definitely I have got phlebitis. What is worse, I have got melancholia. To be in this house alone, ill, is more than I can stand. Ted has been looking after me, nobody else. He has done his best, of course, but his competency about everything practical, and his damned silly talk, has got me down. He asks me directions about things, and then when I begin to tell him, he starts cross-questioning me on my answers. It's most exasperating.

Yesterday I fell into the weeps, and began weeping again first thing this morning. After he had gone through the routine rigmarole about my breakfast tray, I asked him, please to bring me up my bottle of haliveroil capsules. Where were they? They were on the kitchen cabinet. Which room? I exploded. The kitchen cabinet is in the kitchen, of course! I felt furious and sick to death of his silly questions. So I made up my mind not to ask him for anything else, but to get up and attend to myself. I felt crosser and crosser. He should have got a nurse or a woman in to attend to me, anyhow! Not Ted; that costs money. So this morning I finally felt desperate, and as soon as he had left the house, I got up and dressed. I ought not to have done so. I am really ill. My leg is very bad, and Dr. Keighley told him so. That makes no impression on Ted.

Well, when I got downstairs I had a fit of wild weeping. He had re-arranged the kitchen and the dining room. He had turned out my tea wagon and shoved it under the sink; and my little kitchen table he had placed upside down and filled it with crockery. He had been having a clearance. I was enraged, and I burst out crying. However, I pulled myself together and set to work to put everything back in its proper place. I washed up all the dirty crockery about, threw out stale and bad food which had accumulated, cooked some fresh vegetables and made soup. When he came in at one o'clock he was surprised to find me downstairs, and started to order me back to bed. However, I'd had enough of bed and that was that. Then when he went out at two o'clock, I went upstairs, and cleaned and turned out my room. Whilst lying in bed, I had thought out a better way of arranging our room than the way we had it. So this afternoon I simply set to work and re-arranged it. I wanted to clean the room anyhow, as it was filthy dirty, and I moved the furniture myself. It took me three solid hours, but I did it. I was determined I wouldn't ask him anything about it, or to do anything for me.

As a practical man, Ted is simply useless. This house is on my nerves. We have been here two months now, and it is still not to rights. Every job Ted does is badly done. When he lays linoleum, he laps it! I've said nothing about it. I'm just waiting for Artie to come home, and do the job properly. Every job Ted does is like that. Incompetency is his middle name. He thinks he's so smart too! About five weeks ago he threw the garden hose into the little alleyway that leads to the outside toilet, and it lays there, one messy tangle. Several times I have asked him to roll it up on its wheel, and put it away, but no, it's still there, in the way, and has to be walked on by everybody who uses the toilet. All the workmen have been going over it; the carpenter, the plasterer, the bricklayers who have built us a large coal shed, and I twist my ankle on it every time I go round that corner. It might take five minutes to roll it up, but no, it isn't rolled. Then he points out to me a scrubbing brush left in the drain! It isn't my scrubbing brush, anyhow, but belongs to one of the workmen. My God, I'm out of patience.

Well, he's with his beloved brother tonight. I might have remained in bed and he'll still be at Herbert's tonight. Oh, is this a lonesome life! Oh, if I'd only got a daughter, a woman child around! I haven't, so I must look after myself. It is nine o'clock now, and getting dark, so I will go and re-bandage my leg for the night before it's time for the blackout. The Germans continue raiding us nightly. They dropped incendiary bombs in Harold Wood two nights ago. Oh this damned war; that gets us down too. Au-revoir.

- *SUNDAY, AUGUST 4,1940* -

Twenty-six years ago today Great Britain entered the last war. Six thirty p.m. and it is a warm sunny evening. Ted is out at church. I have been downstairs all day today and feel much better for it. I am apparently no worse for my furniture shifting yesterday, though I have two big purple bruises on my arm. I must have hurt myself without realizing it. My ankle is drying up considerable, but the phlebitis patch is swollen and inflamed as ever. However, in my spirits I feel fine. Bed was getting me down. I am now going to fix up my bed and listen to the London Symphony Orchestra, conducted by Sir Henry Wood, playing the "Pathetique" at seven fifty.

Here is what I purchased at Bumpus: Beard: *Rise of American Civilization*, Wright: *Hawkers and Walkers in Early America*, Emerson: *Works: Complete in 4 volumes,* Melina Rorke: *Memoirs of the 90's in South Africa*, Landor: *Classical Conversations,* Undset: *Stages on the Road*. I am delighted with this lot.

- *MONDAY, AUGUST 5, 1940* -

It should be a bank holiday, but it isn't. I wrote to Cuthie and keep choking with laughter at something I consider very funny. When I shuffled my room around on Saturday, of course I had to shift and re-hang the pictures. Because I couldn't quite make up my mind to where to hang it, I did not re-hang the crucifix, but left it on Ted's bureau. Well, he has hung it plumb over the middle of the head of the bed. This, I know, is the traditional position for it in Catholic families. I have always kept ours away from that spot. I have put it in obscure places: behind the door, or in a recess, or beside Ted's mirror. When one considers what goes on in the connubial bed, the wall behind and above it seems to me the most inappropriate place possible ever to hang a crucifix. Such a position for such an article just strikes me as funny. Hope I don't giggle some night soon when Ted wants to be a loving husband.

- *TUESDAY, AUGUST 6, 1940* -

Dr. Keighley says I may now put a new viscopaste on my bad leg, and she will see it again in a week's time. I am still to rest as much as possible. I am not to put on my shoes, nor walk about the house more than is absolutely necessary. So I'm still to play Madame Recamier on the sofa. I had a cheery leaflet put in the letterbox this morning: our orders what to do in case of invasion. The authorities seem certain the Germans will attempt invasion during the next week or fortnight. My God! When is this crazy war going to end!

There is a rumor today, via Reuter, that Julius Streicher is dead. Supposedly executed by Goring's order. Streicher was the notorious Nazi Jew baiter. I am sure the world hopes he is dead; hopes all the Nazi's meet violent death, at the hands of their "friends." Pray God they do taste in themselves their own brutalities and betrayals.

EPISODE #15

- WEDNESDAY, AUGUST 7, 1940 -

The sound of bombs and guns all morning, and an air raid warning at eleven o'clock. No damage in Romford.

Started with a new charlady today, a much younger woman than Mrs. Bull. Mrs. Rose Whitan, who is Mrs. Fardell's daughter. The house certainly looks better for her ministrations.

Provoked at lunch by Ted's criticisms. In the pantry there was the remains of Sunday's leg of lamb, of which we were tired, and a gammon rasher of ham, some leftover stewed plums, of which Ted hasn't eaten any. So, I served lunch as follows: the gammon rasher baked with some Heinz beans; a dish of pilaf, with plenty of onions and tomatoes; some canned pears, and coffee. Ted said the rasher was tough, and I could have it. The pears he remarked, "Why tinned fruit? Don't you know you should serve fresh fruit these days? You certainly are a bum housekeeper!"

Now it would have been no good offering him the cold lamb. He refused that the last time it came to table. He also refuses stewed plums; moreover, I didn't want red plums after red tomatoes; and as for the cold rice pudding, naturally I wouldn't serve that after pilaf, which is basically rice. So I served nice white tinned pears.

Actually tinned fruit is cheaper than fresh, provided you could get any fresh! Cherries, strawberries, currants, and raspberries are finished. Melons, blackberries, and apples are not in yet. Bananas haven't been seen for weeks. Oranges are three pence apiece. Lemons are offered at ten pence—ten pence!—apiece, and eating apples, if you can find them, are a shilling a pound. So what?

Even in today's paper correspondents are writing in to complain of the high price of fruit, and asking can't something be done about it; and one woman actually stated it was cheaper to buy tinned fruit than fresh. At least the tinned fruit is sweet. The sugar ration is eight ounces per week per person. Therefore in this house one pound of sugar per week is all I can get. There is no fruit. There is no sugar to stew it with, even if we could get fruit. At this time, there are no imports, which accounts for the lack of bananas and citrus fruits, but the dealers are profiteering on all homegrown produce. In spite of government control, the cost of living has increased by at least fifty percent since the beginning of the war. Ted says I'm a bum housekeeper! Well maybe I am, but I do get damn tired of his comments. I didn't answer him. What was the good?

- *THURSDAY, AUGUST 15, 1940* -

The Feast of the Assumption

I don't care a damn about what feast it is. I am full of the most awful anger. All night I was awake with the airplanes passing and passing overhead. No alarm was sounded, but I expected one every minute. Ted lay peacefully sleeping. I lay cursing. I cursed Hitler, I cursed the war, I cursed all the old politicians, and all the blah-blahing jingoists;

I cursed all men for what they have brought the world to; and I cursed my man for what he has brought me to, and brought to the twins also. God damn men, I say, and he is doing so; but in their damnation we women are damned too, and double damned; we are all not only cursed by nature, but we are cursed by the world the men impose upon us, and then bring about our ears. What do I care for the fairy tales of Theology? I care nothing, not a farthing. I hate men and all their romances.

- *FRIDAY, AUGUST 16, 1940* -

I am steadier today, but with a ruthless mind. I was full of visitors yesterday. Mrs. Jude came in on her way from the late mass (which Ted had been playing—'playing' in more senses than one, I think), and stayed to lunch. Then before she left, early in the afternoon, Irene White arrived with the baby Bernadette; and before she left Mrs. Ryle called, and also stayed to tea. We talked about eternal life ideas of my own.

Then at half past seven in the evening, the air raid warning was given. It's very terrifying. Ted was painting the bathroom, but came down and said he supposed he ought to go down to his shelter. I exclaimed, "Oh don't go, don't leave me!" and then I got a harangue. He didn't go, saying that since it was only open until eight o'clock, and since it was Thursday and so there wouldn't be many people about on South Street, and it would be eight o'clock before he could get there—still, he began to scold me. He scolded until the all clear. He said I was a very selfish woman, and that there were other people to be saved besides me. He said I was a fool if I couldn't be left alone, and he said to be frightened was silly. One ought to control one's fear.

I gave up. I give up. I feel I hate him, more and more. He does not see his own selfishness; but if ever any person pursued undeviatingly his or her own desire, that person is Edward Thompson.

These past weeks I have really been very ill. He hasn't realized it at all. I have suffered intense pain, and great loneliness. To be left alone ill in bed, day after day, was unbearable. He didn't even get a nurse to look after me. I couldn't bear it, up there all alone. I longed for my children. I do long for my children. I should be in the midst of them, where they could come to look after me in my need, and where I could take occasional pleasure in their presence, ill or well. No, Ted has arranged things differently. When I look at the baby Bernadette running around the house, I feel that my little granddaughters should also be able to come in and run around; and when I think of Cuthie and Artie caught up in this devilish war, I think that too is Ted's fault and I hate him for all the deprivation and sorrow he has brought upon me, so he thinks it is his duty to go and stand guard over the passing strangers who may enter a shelter; and my duty to sit alone while he does so. My terror, which I cannot help, is of no account. So I think, where are my children? Where are my children! I am alone, sickly alone.

All this week the air raids have been intensifying. Yesterday's raids were the heaviest yet. Over a thousand German planes attacked us, in nine different attacks. Report says we brought down one hundred and forty-four of them. Oh hell! Hell for all of us and for all the boys in the air too, British or German. All this is the work of men's minds and men's hands. I say curse such works of men, and all men's crazy ideas. War! What sense is there in war?

Would women make war? No. Women are realists. Women know the cost of life. They preserve it, save it, and heal it. It is women who know what love is, and it is women who love; not men, they can only hate and destroy. Yet they see themselves as heroes. My God!

At twelve thirty p.m. the siren sounded. I closed and darkened the windows, lowered the gas in the oven, and sat in Auntie Daisy's rocker in the corner of the dining room to wait for the all clear. This did not sound 'til one twenty p.m. Soon after half past, Ted came in smiling and very pleased with himself. He told me about the wonderful good conduct of all the people in his air-raid shelter. He said there were about one hundred and seventy-five men, women, and children, all "very good." He added, "You see, you're alright. Nothing has happened to you." Yes, I'm all right, but something has happened to me.

I do not expect Ted to come home to me during daytime raids. I know he has pledged himself to take charge of a shelter between the hours of eight am and eight p.m. I do expect him to be here with me at night. Last night the warning startled me, and involuntarily I asked him not to leave me. This, in his eyes, was a crime. He did not stay with me because I asked him to, but because by the time he could have changed his clothes and got to the shelter, the time would have been after eight p.m. To be alone in danger at night is particularly frightening, and the fact that the mere bodily presence of another human being can give comfort and courage is something he cannot understand and doesn't want to understand, he says. I say he is cold-blooded, and not human. He is proud of his insensibility; he thinks that shows his superior intelligence. "Use your mind, Lady! Use your mind!"

Does he suppose I want to be frightened? I do use my mind, otherwise I should lose it. What I suffer is pure animal fright. It is the old primitive woman in me who knows she has reason to be scared, and she acts without waiting for directions from my head. She acts scared, in the very pit of my stomach, and I can't control her, either; she knows danger better than I do, and she pays no attention whatsoever to my educated reason. She didn't panic quite so much today because it was mid-day perhaps, with bright sun shining. How queer it was afterwards to pull back the curtains and see the serene and shining day!

Nor did I pray so much today, not in the same way as in the dark nights. I called more simply on God. God be with me! God be with me! I tried to pray to Mary, Queen of Heaven, and on the instant knew that such an invocation had become empty for me. On the instant I saw that my Catholicism had dropped from me, like the dead skin, which curls and drops from my leg each day. I'm back where I was forty years ago, in a pure Theism. That is what happened to me. My God is an impersonal principle: the Light, Life, Love, and Goodness that Jesus used to talk about. God is a spirit, and my spirit was calling to spirit, and that is all it can call to. To me all the historical fact, true or fancied of religion, is only a great hindrance. Persons confuse me and weary me. I do not even think of God as Father. The fathers I have known have not been very effective men. I certainly do not think of Mary, Mother of God. For I am a mother myself, and I know the limitations of mothers. Such ideas of religion are not adult enough for me. To what person that I know, or know of, could I appeal? Not one. For there is not one person in this world that I could ever feel to be, let alone acknowledge being, my superior. I can only look to myself, the God within, my principle.

As for Catholicism, I do not feel impelled to disown or disavow it. The practice of the Catholic religion is a performance, which I can perform, and will perform, as far as I am able, for as long as Ted and I have to continue to live together. I can go through the motions. Inside:

inside nothing can make me believe, nothing can give me that faith. I am a natural born heretic, and nothing, not even love, policy, or war, can convince me against my own convictions. I can conform, can bow down in the house of Rimmion, but my inner secret self is free, and will be free, no matter how persuasively I try to put her into shackles.

Sitting there in the dark, waiting for the chance of death, which might descend on me at any moment, I saw all this. Sitting there waiting, wondering if I should ever see my children again, it was a wait at the bar of death, and I saw myself, without any pretenses, as the woman I am. It is the woman I have always been, a woman with a practical mind, a free spirit, and a rational soul; essentially individual, and asserting my own terms, my own woman's terms against my world and my life, as I have to live it. Men's terms, men's reason, men's rulings, men's arguments, are not for me. I see what men's works are, and know that I could do better. No man, ancient or modern, dead or living, is going to dictate to me; not to my free mind, my free soul. A husband, the man's made world I cannot shake loose from, may constrain my person and my movements, but myself, inviolably myself, and men's religions hold no validity for me.

I have just been attending to the dustman. He tells me they are all collecting "dust." He was enthusiastic about our air force, and spoke of the raid over Croydon last night. He thought this mid-day's raid must have been at Croydon as the guns sounded that far away. He also told me, "One of our chaps lost his wife last night because of the siren. When that sounded she just dropped down dead. Just dropped down dead." That's what fright can do to a woman.

Ted jeers, and asks, "What is there to be afraid of?" Pain and fire, anxiety for those who belong to us and are exposed directly to danger, mutilation, suffocation, and sudden death; that's what is to be afraid of.

It is now seven forty-five p.m. Ted has just left for church. He says he will be late returning because he has a meeting in the presbytery afterwards.

The King has made an announcement that he desires Sunday, September eighth, to be observed by all as a day of prayer. President Roosevelt, likewise, for the same Sunday. Why pray?

Nations go to war because they will war. God does not inflict war upon the world so why ask him to stop it? As war is waged by the collective will, it is the longest enduring will that will win it. Having once started a war, men must fight 'til they beat or are beaten. To petition Jehovah to bless the battle is to return to the mentality of the Bronze Age. When men no longer desire war they will cease to wage it. Why ask God to save us? We must cease being stupid and save ourselves.

At five fifteen p.m. we had another warning, and the all clear did not sound until an hour afterwards. There was more noise and more planes overhead than at mid-day. This time I did not pray at all. Instead I felt myself suffused with anger that men can be such fools. What good does a war do? Men destroying each other, and reporting it like a sport too! It makes me wild. It is the greatest senseless folly men ever commit. God, how I hate all fool men! War is the worst terror and destruction in the world. I hate it, beyond everything.

Yet there are some fools who declare it is the punishment of God for the sins of the nations. To me this is sheer blasphemy. God does not ordain war; man ordains it. Men will have it so, and when they will not have it so, then and only then, will it cease to occur.

Yesterday when I was clearing out an old basket of rubbish for the garbage man I found an old New York publication, which was most illuminating for today. The Literary Digest put it out in 1922. It is "an Atlas of the New Europe and the Far East, showing the new countries and new boundaries resulting from the Great War and from the Treaties of Peace with Explanatory Historical, Political, and Economic articles prepared from the most recent and authoritative sources in Europe and America."

Studying these maps, it is easy to see why Germany finally began on her campaign of aggression and why Russia, Hungary, Italy, follow suit. The settlement of Europe after the Great War was hugely vindictive, and naturally unreasonable. That settlement should have been unsettled long ago. But no! Nothing sensible! They have kept tight hold on the loot. Everything Hitler had been asking for could have adjusted by good will, brains, and justice. I believe that when he said he wanted peace, he meant it. He was fobbed off and fobbed off. So he took what he wanted in the end, and he has taken it by force, cunning and violence. The old statesmen of Europe are to blame for this war primarily, damn them. My God, will men ever really live by reason and justice!

EPISODE #16

- SATURDAY, AUGUST 17, 1940 -

A quiet day: no warnings. I read an article in the *Times* today about the "indifference" of the French. This does not surprise me. I'm sure the French never really wanted to go into this war. They hadn't been attacked. They were tired of war, not fully recovered from the Great War of fourteen yet. Why should they fight for the Poles? So too I think it was with our men in France. Why fight for the French, or the Belgians? Now that they have come home, they will fight for home. Any man can see why he should defend his own land, but it is not so easy to see why he should fight to defend the land of the foreigner.

- SUNDAY, AUGUST 18, 1940 -

A warning at one o'clock today, which lasted an hour and another at six o'clock, which lasted forty minutes. Report is that the Germans have destroyed Croyden.

- *MONDAY, AUGUST 19, 1940* -

Yesterday's was the worst raid of the war yet. Croyden is practically wiped out. No major raids today. Very tired. The strain of the raids is exhausting.

- *TUESDAY, AUGUST 20, 1940* -

Artie came home last night. We were just going up to bed, about ten thirty p.m. when he knocked at the door. He has three days leave.

- *THURSDAY, AUGUST 22, 1940* -

It is ten forty-five p.m. and I am alone in the house and rather nervous. Artie left at six thirty p.m. to return to camp. Ted left at two thirty p.m. to take a walking holiday with George Butcher. We have had no raids or warnings in this district today, but yesterday the Germans bombed Brentwood, which is very close. Last Monday they bombed North Weald, which perhaps is even closer. Last week they hit in Herald Wood. Anyhow, here I am alone in the house, and have got to get through the nights somehow. The nine o'clock news was very alarming. We were told that today the Germans bombed our convoy in the channel from the coast of France; they have long-range guns along the coast from Boulogne to Calais, and they bombed our ships all along the way to Dover. Dover was shaken! They also bombed the convoy from the air. What next? They have now reached London several times. Last week they got Wimbledon, as well as Croydon.

Anyhow, I've got to go to bed. I got Artie to change my furniture around again before he went out this morning.

I had him place my bed behind the door, and with its head against the inner wall. That position seems a trifle safer to me than the position it was in before. Though actually, of course, no spot is safe if a bomb actually hits you. Whole houses fall down six at a time, so what does it signify where the bed is? Of course I know I am in no more danger without Ted than with him. Nevertheless I am frightened to be left alone in this house. I've got to endure the loneliness and the fright. I might overcome the situation with a strong whiskey, but I don't dare do that, because if I slept too soundly I shouldn't hear a warning if it sounded. So all I can do is act valiant and pray. So goodnight. I keep telling myself I've got to go to bed, so I really had better go there. So goodnight, goodnight! God keep me!

- *FRIDAY, AUGUST 23, 1940* -

It is eleven p.m. Ted telephoned from Oxford about a half hour ago. He said he was having a good time. He also gave me Butcher's number and asked me to ring Mrs. Butcher and tell her where they were and that Georgie was well and having a good time. Of course I had to say I would, but somehow or other this request made me flash with anger. Why the devil, I thought, couldn't Georgie telephone his mother for himself! After all, he's considerably over thirty years old! Maybe he wanted to save the price of a phone call. Anyhow, I think it's cheek.

I was very near to anger all day anyhow. The sirens sounded at three thirty a.m. this morning and I had to come down in the dark and sit alone in the house 'til the raid passed, which was four ten a.m., much noise of guns and machines. We heard later today that the bombs fell in Edmonton, wrecking a cinema and a church, as well as several houses. Again tonight we had a raid. The siren sounded at nine thirty but the all clear came at ten p.m. When I told Ted of the day's two attacks, he only asked, "Any damage done?"

- *SATURDAY, AUGUST 24, 1940* -

We have had two raids in this locality already today. The first came at eight thirty this morning, and lasted 'til nine twenty. The second came at eleven twenty and lasted 'til eleven forty-five. Mr. Shea was here during the second one, fixing the radio for me. I've had it shifted from the parlor to the dining room. In this house we have no second loud speaker, so that to hear the radio whilst in the dining room it was necessary to leave both the parlor and the dining room doors open. This is not so bad in summertime, but as the weather cools it is not pleasant, especially as the little hall and the front door intervene, providing plenty of draught.

Young Shea saw the raiders last night. He said they looked to him to be over Abridge. Wherever they were the explosions shook this town. When Ted phoned me at ten thirty last night my heart was still galloping from the fright they gave me an hour before. Yesterday, too, Dover and Folkstone were gunned from the French coast. Over one hundred shells were delivered from Corp Gres Key. War. Man's game.

It is five p.m. The third raid of the day has just finished. The siren blew at three thirty and before I could close the windows and pull down the shades the bombs began falling. This has been the worst raid we have had so far. I expected this house to be struck at any minute. There were two terrific blasts, which sounded as though they had got the station, or the hospital. What a day for it to happen! A Saturday afternoon with the town crowded with all the Saturday shoppers!

It is now six p.m. Edna Renacre has just been in to see if I was alright. She said there were eight German machines over Romford. Our spitfires went up to attack and the duels could be watched from South Street. She said she saw two machines brought down towards Rainham and three large open ambulances full of bodies on stretchers going towards the hospital. The last bomb fell at Upminster, on the railroad, and when she went into Romford Station a few minutes ago to buy her season ticket, a board was being put up, stating that all services to Upminister and Elm Park were suspended. South Street, Eastern Road, this Western Road, and Carlton Road are full of scattered shrapnel.

It is ten thirty p.m. Getting sleepy but afraid to go up to bed. The nine o'clock news said that a continuous air-battle has been going on all over England all day. Guns from the French coast have also been shelling over South coast intermittently, destroying property and causing casualties. Ramsgate has been severely damaged. Here the gas works were set afire. The machines over Romford were apparently part of a group of fifty, which were making for London.

Elizabeth Coppen phoned me this evening that Clem and her husband were at South Weald this afternoon and ran into a terrific battle overhead. They had to get out of their car and lay in the ditch. They had a six-month-old baby with them!

The news said we brought down thirty-four machines and lost ten, but one of our pilots was safe. One! This is God damned ghastly awful. I am furious. I grow angrier and angrier.

No news from Ted today. Just as I wrote this the phone rang. It was Ted, phoning from Reading. He says he will be home some time tomorrow afternoon. No raids where he was. He sounded half-drunk to me but perhaps it was only the transmission. "Take care of yourself," he said. Yes, by God, I have to!

- SUNDAY, AUGUST 25, 1940 -

I have just been listening to the morning's news. It stated that eight hundred German bombers, escorted by an equal number of fighters, attacked us in the afternoon yesterday. Three hundred, with their escorts, attacked the London area, five hundred, with their fighters, the Portsmouth area. Our group overhead right here consisted of thirty bombers with about thirty escorting fighters. Except saying that forty-nine of the bombers were brought down, no other estimates of losses, either the German's or ours, was given. This is rather ominous, I think.

Then, again, late last night we had another raid. It lasted from eleven thirty p.m. to one thirty a.m. this morning. This was directed to London. An incendiary started a large fire there in a commercial building. It was brought under control. Nonetheless the announcer added that, very promptly, for a quarter of a mile in every direction, the streets were crowded with our firemen and machines and fire-fighting apparatus, and the whole neighborhood closed to the public. What is one to think? This was no little fire, confined to one commercial building, was it?

When the late siren went last night the Thomson's from next door came in here to sit with me. They stayed until two o'clock in the morning. I think this was very kind. When I saw Mrs. Thomson yesterday morning she was very surprised to learn I had been alone the previous night, and later in the afternoon she came to tell me, "Jack says if there is a raid tonight he is coming in to sit with you. He was awfully shocked to hear you were alone last night. So remember, don't get frightened. If there's a warning tonight, we're coming in to sit with you. That's sure. John says you shan't be alone if he can help it." So they came, very promptly, too. They laid the child on the sofa, and we sat together round the fire, chatting.

I was glad, for I was sick with nervousness. John Thomson persisted in talking, and every time the explosions shook the windows he just sat calmly ignoring the battle, and talking, talking, telling stories, reminiscing. He was very helpful. So different from my man, who, if he had been here, would have been tish-tashing about, snappy with impatience, and cursing the Germans for disturbing his sleep. Yes, that's how it would have been.

Now I want to go upstairs and dress. Edna said she would come in to lunch with me today, "so that I shouldn't be alone." That is kind of the girl. I have to do my leg too. It is very bad again this morning, with inflammation and swelling spread up the leg again from where it had receded, and open and throbbing with pain at the ankle. Nerves, I suppose.

I shall not write in here again today. Edna will be here at noon, and Ted will probably arrive around teatime.

Last Sunday the Germans got Croydon. I wonder what they will get today! Sunday is their favorite day for destruction. So Au-revoir.

EPISODE #17

- TUESDAY, AUGUST 27, 1940 -

It is ten a.m. and I am feeling very wonky. The German's were raiding over London for six hours last night; our Romford sirens blew at ten thirty p.m. and the all clear did not come 'til three thirty this morning. Consequently, no sleep, so very tired. On Sunday the first raid did not come 'til ten thirty p.m., and lasted one hour. The next came as we were settling to sleep at quarter to one, but this one only lasted half an hour; then we had nothing 'til half past three yesterday afternoon. I had only just got into the house, returning from the doctor's. This raid lasted 'til four fifty p.m. and was a bad one.

This week's report from the doctor was not so good. Inflammation and swelling has spread up my leg again, and I have put on weight instead of losing any. I have put on nearly two pounds since last week. Last week I had lost four. Doctor says this is probably water gain accumulated in my leg. I think so too. On Sunday night during the raid I was suddenly aware of water trickling down inside my bandages. This is nerves and shock, of course.

On to nerves, I can add an exasperated frame of mind. Ted is not a bit of help in an emergency, far from it. He just talks his silly talk until I could scream. I don't scream, of course, but I feel so exasperated and annoyed inside, it can't possibly do any good. I just look at him and think him one blasted fool. He is. His contentiousness and disputatiousness wears away on my patience. Talk! Talk! He will talk. He is so scathing and thinks he is so clever! I think he is merely very rude. He was up and out to church this morning just as usual. What good does that do, either him or God Almighty? When he comes back he criticizes me because the fire is out. I hadn't touched the fire. I had noticed that the drafts were opened, so presumed he was attending to it. He had opened the drafts, but he said I was responsible for the fire.

I said, "I thought you were attending to the fire."

Then he was off. He said, "Think! Yes, you would think! And all your thoughts are wrong! That's the trouble with you. You don't use your head properly. You haven't got brains. You've only got scrambled eggs in your brain box. You presume to think what the other fellow's doing, and you're all wrong. Why don't you use your head properly? Use the intelligence God gave you."

He was in the little hall by this time, but he came back into the room to add, witheringly, "That is, if you've got any!"

I am not withered. I merely think he is colossally rude, but I don't even tell him so. What I know is that I got one of those sickening flashes of knowledge by which I see how acutely I dislike this person. I think: well, he's tired. The raids do try him also, though he'll never admit to that, and he has to nag, because he has a nagging disposition, and I'm simply the unlucky being who happens to stand before him. So I say nothing, and look nothing, but Oh God I'm weary!

First raid warning, nine thirty p.m. 'til midnight. Then had just got into bed and settled for sleep when the warning sounded again, twelve thirty a.m., all-clear one fifteen a.m., of tomorrow the 28th.

My physical woman is cracking with fatigue, and my inner woman is splitting with laughter. Last night the first warning of the day sounded at nine p.m., just as the news was beginning, and the all-clear did not come until four o'clock this morning. This has been the longest raid of the war so far, and it was general all over England. We have not been told yet what damage has been done, but should think it must be considerable. There was plenty around here by the sound of things. There were two nearby explosions around two o'clock when I thought our house was shattered, and I surely thought the front door was blown in. However, we're intact. Moreover, Ted never heard these bombs. He had fallen asleep on the rug before the fire, and I had to wake him when the all clear came.

I did not sleep at all but, as the hours wore on, I began to suffer with my leg. I was in the corner rocker, which is my usual station, but sitting up so long with my leg in the downward position, I could feel it growing heavier and heavier with blood and it began to swell and ache with constriction. Finally I ventured into the parlor and found a hassock and a cushion, and came back to the rocker and propped my leg up like an old man with the gout. It is not safe to lie on the sofa during a raid, as that is right in direct line with the window, and I don't think there is any other possible position for it in this room. It is a fine place for reading in peace times, but highly dangerous in any blast.

Last night I did not pray at all. My God has got nothing to do with this war. This war is going on because men will have it. Why bother God to stop something we can stop for ourselves as soon as we have the will to peace? As for seeking for personal safety, I no longer want to do it. In the first raids in June I was terrified and I invoked God and the Virgin and all the saints of Heaven to protect me. Not now. Since then I have overcome that childish primitive fear and I feel as safe with God as has always been natural for me. I do really trust the power of God and believe in his protection, so why bother him with little petitions? That's so childish. It is like a child with the 'gim-me'. My instinct is to thank, praise, and adore my God, not to ask for favors.

As for the Virgin and the saints and angels, they've all come unstuck for me. So has all theology. What in the world is theology except men talking? Guessing about ultimates? Well, I can talk for myself and guess for myself; in fact, I do, and with my woman's mind and from my woman's viewpoint and I simply don't accept the men's say so. Men!

What is greatly wrong with the world is man's wrong thinking, so why think men's thoughts? Well, I don't, and I don't tend to try anymore either. I'll find truth for myself, thank you. Truth isn't men's prerogative, nor women's either, and I'm looking for truth, not doctrine.

This is why I am laughing. After several hours of being in the front line, with bloody destruction apt to annihilate us at any moment, exhausted with fatigue when the danger ceased for the night, we finally went upstairs to bed soon after four this morning. Then, around five o'clock, Ted took me for loving. This struck me as so incongruous and silly, I had to put compulsion on myself not to bust into laughing. A man's lust is ridiculous, and his sex hunger is the greatest thing in his life, stronger than death, war, and imminent destruction. Behind it all, the woman is so impersonal to him. He does not love her for herself, or for her sake, but simply and purely for his own need. Oh men! Well then, at seven he rose as per usual and went out to mass. I laugh and laugh. Talk about unbalanced minds, talk about soppy romantics, talk about the self-centered and the self-willed, the egotists; surely Ted is one of these prize fools!

Ted had just gone out to mass, and I am waiting for the kettle to boil so that I can get a cup of tea. Yesterday I lived through what has been the most terrifying day of my life. Today may be even worse. We were raided six times yesterday, starting at half past eight in the morning, with the last raid at eleven thirty until midnight. Then at twelve fifty-five this morning they came again, and the all clear was not sounded 'til three fifty-five this morning. So already we have had the first raid of today. The whole week has been full of raids, with an average of four a day, but yesterday surpassed all, in number and in intensity. Ted got no meals yesterday. The first warning went as he was ready for breakfast. He did not return to the house, as we had a second alarm at ten forty. He came in looking for lunch at twelve fifty and at twelve fifty-five the siren went again, and off he had to dash to his shelter. When we were starting to eat just after five thirty p.m. the sirens went again! Then we were raided at seven fifty p.m. and again after eleven fifty p.m.

The raids at one p.m. and five thirty are the worst Romford has yet experienced. At midday fifteen bombs were dropped in the very center of town. The first one fell in Victoria Road, only missing the railway bridge by a half block. Then in a straight line across all those little roads towards Hornchurch and the Romeo, fourteen others were dropped, demolishing shops and houses and killing many people. Rumor gave the estimate dead as fifty, but we do not know the actual number yet. Perhaps it was more. I sat alone here in the most awful terror I have ever known. The noise was devilish; the house shook so much I expected it to fall upon me, and the suction in this air is indescribable. Machines were dwelling right over the house, and each bomb as it fell sounded as though it might be in the back garden.

It lasted for an hour and I thought every moment was my last. I prayed as I never prayed in my life before. Not calmly, thinking about what I was saying, but wildly, incessantly, petitioning like any frantic child, God be with me! Jesus save me! Mary save me! Joseph save me! God be with me! God be with me!

Well, he was. I am still alive. In that hour, terror I had no mind, no intellect. I simply called on God and all the saints I knew, the angels and the whole hierarchy of Heaven to save me. I wasn't a mind or a person, considering, deliberating. I was a frightened human atom, calling on my Gods. The greater the terror and helplessness the stronger flared my faith. In that awful hour I believed The Faith as I have never believed it before, even when I thought I did. Today I still believe. I must. Reason has got nothing to do with it. Belief is instinct. Perhaps it was yesterday that was the day of my real conversion.

Now I am going to dress ready for the day. I expect it will be a bad day. It is this Sunday a year ago that the war started. Anyhow the Germans would rather war on a Sunday than any other day of the week. Last Sunday, Artie wrote us, there was no church parade for the army. Our men stand ready every instant for the defense. With God, they will save England. How many young men must die today? Oh, God help us!

- *WEDNESDAY, SEPTEMBER 4, 1940* -

First raid today, nine twenty a.m. to nine forty-five a.m. Gladys arrived unexpectedly about eleven o'clock. She has gone very thin. She has lost over three stone since June. We had a warning whilst over lunch. It lasted from one twenty p.m. to one forty-five p.m. Gladys left about five, as she wanted to get back to Hammersmith before the evening raids began. She has put Aunty Daisy into a nursing home for two weeks whilst she has a holiday. She plans to return to Plymouth next Monday.

Our other raids today: nine p.m. until ten fifty p.m. Eleven fifteen p.m. until midnight.

- *THURSDAY, SEPTEMBER 5, 1940* -

The raids are increasing, lasting longer, and much more violent. Today's list is twelve thirty a.m. 'til three am, calling us from bed. Ten fifty a.m. until eleven a.m.; three ten p.m. 'til four forty p.m.; nine ten p.m. 'til five a.m. (tomorrow, Friday the 6th).

- *FRIDAY, SEPTEMBER 6, 1940* -

Raids worse and worse. After spending the night downstairs, we finally went up to bed at five a.m. when the all clear sounded. At five twenty in the morning the alarm came again, so we went downstairs at once. The raid lasted until six a.m. Then more raids followed throughout the day. When the all clear came at eleven twenty p.m. we went up to bed, but before we could settle to sleep the warning came again at eleven forty-five. It cleared at one instead of five, so we were able to get a little sleep. We did not wake until seven twenty, still downstairs, but Ted dressed in five minutes, and rushed off to seven thirty mass anyhow. Such enthusiasm! I believe. I have faith. I certainly haven't got that urgent need to go to church. I can pray at home.

This morning finds us smiling anyhow. I think Ted is one of the funniest men in the world. Last night when we went up to bed at eleven thirty he wanted to love. I couldn't. The siren went and I went cold. Ted was surprised! "You don't mean to say you lose feeling! Oh, don't let that happen. Don't let Hitler kill your pleasure for you. You don't mean to say he can? You're frightened? You don't want to be loved? You want to get downstairs? Oh, Lady, what a shame! Oh, curse Hitler! Damn him!"

Funny, isn't it? This morning he rushed to mass. Yes, the Thompson men do what they want to do all right. I was reading an article in the *Times* Literary Supplement today, on Wilfred Blunt. The writer commented: "he [Blunt] could never accept that it was an abiding law that nothing is constant but change, nothing sure but love and death."

I thought to myself: What love? Love to man means coition, and nothing else; and he will have it, even though the bombs are raining from the heavens. Oh, men are funny. It is a good job women can laugh at them.

- SATURDAY, SEPTEMBER 7, 1940 -

First raid, very violent indeed: five fifty p.m. 'til six forty p.m. There was death again dropping on the crowds of Saturday shoppers. Second raid, started at eight thirty-five p.m., continued without ceasing until five in the morning of Sunday.

- SUNDAY, SEPTEMBER 8, 1940 -

Last night's raid on London was the worst yet. Ted and I cowered here in this little dining room. Ted pulled the couch into the corner, so I could keep my legs up. They get so bad when I sit, holding them down for hours. He rolled himself into a blanket, and lay on a cushion spread on the floor. Several times I thought we were surely destroyed. I prayed and prayed, and here we are still alive, and a roof still over us. The radio announcer told us that the raiders had concentrated on London, especially the East End and the riverbanks. Our R.A.F. brought down ninety-nine German machines, but our civilian casualties are grave, over four hundred killed, and between one hundred and fourteen hundred severely injured. One bomb fell into a shelter holding one thousand people! Several bad fires have started. This has been the worst raid of the war so far, and London has suffered tremendously. Oh God help us!

Our first raid today did not come 'til twelve thirty in the afternoon and was comparatively short, ceasing at one twenty-five p.m.; our next, and last, still proceeding, began of Monday the ninth at eight five p.m., nearly an hour earlier than their usual evening start. Raid ended at five thirty-five a.m.

It was another night of terror. Ted rolls up on the floor and can even fall asleep. I lie on the sofa and tremble from top to toe. The situation is completely frightful, and we are only on the fringe of it. What the actual hell further into London must be, God knows.

It is eleven fifteen a.m. now, Monday the ninth, no figures yet available. No raids so far today. The sky is clouding at last! If only the rain would fall, that would be a blessing. Most awful fires are raging in the city; I don't know how man can cope with them. Oh God, send us rain! I don't know what has happened in Hammersmith. According to the radio, most of the damage has been further into the center of the city, and at the docks.

- MONDAY, SEPTEMBER 9, 1940 -

First raid five ten p.m. 'til six twenty-five p.m., second raid eight forty p.m., lasting 'til five fifty a.m. of Tuesday the tenth. This is the worst raid yet. City badly hit.

- TUESDAY, SEPTEMBER 10, 1940 -

We had five more raids lasting from midafternoon until five in the morning. These night raids are worse and worse. They are concentrated on London, and doing great damage, and killing many civilians. Everything is Hell.

EPISODE #18

- WEDNESDAY, SEPTEMBER 11, 1940 -

We had raids lasting on and off from midmorning until the following day.

- THURSDAY, SEPTEMBER 12, 1940 -

Three twenty p.m. No raid so far today. Yesterday's afternoon raid on London was the heaviest yet, but we brought down eighty-nine German Machines, to our own loss of only twenty-seven. Last night's raid was a little less successful than the other night raids for the Germans, because we had brought heavier anti-aircraft guns into action, and their bombers could not get through so well as the other nights. There was just as much damage done in Aldgate East, London. Yesterday afternoon they got Buckingham Palace! This week London has suffered tremendously. Huge fires at the docks, Eastham, Bow, Poplar, Whitechapel, Bethnal Green, Bishopsgate, several London hospitals, churches and museums, railway stations, schools, workhouses, shops, factories; devastation seems to be endless. St. Paul's churchyard, Cheapside, The Bank, Regent Street. No rain. Today a strong wind is blowing, but the moon won't be at the equinox until the 21st and 22nd.

The Britton and Londoner are not terrorized. He is simply coldly angry, and more determined than ever to lick Hitler and his Nazi's. The devil himself can't frighten an Englishman.

I am frightened. Many bombs have fallen here in Romford and nearby, houses are stuck into heaps, and people killed. I lie in the corner and pray. That's all I can do. Last night the gunfire was simply terrific. The din itself scares you. We were told this morning that it was our heavier guns in action, and that they were effective in checking the German onslaught.

- *FRIDAY, SEPTEMBER 13, 1940* -

Our last night warning was sounded at nine ten p.m. and the all clear did not come until five fifty a.m. this morning. The rest of this day's raids: seven forty a.m. to eight thirty-five a.m.; nine fifty a.m. to two p.m. This was a terrific bombardment of London. Amongst the targets hit was Buckingham Palace. Four p.m. to four twenty p.m.

- *SATURDAY, SEPTEMBER 14, 1940* -

Our last warning yesterday sounded at nine p.m. The all clear was not given until five fifty-five a.m. this morning. Seven more raids today.

- *SUNDAY, SEPTEMBER 15, 1940* -

I had an hour of inexplicable exquisite happiness this morning. First of all I had a good sleep in bed, the first for a long time. When the all clear came at three thirty this morning, I decided to go up to bed, and hope for two undisturbed hours, in coolness and comfort. I slept alone until seven o'clock, when Ted came up and began to dress for church. He goes to church every morning, raids or no raids.

Then after breakfast I had time to get a good bath and dress in all fresh clothes, such a treat! Then the day was wonderful, bright and sharp and clear, one of those astringent autumnal days, which I have always loved. I put on a dress I had never worn before, a dark blue crepe I bought at Pontings last year. When I came downstairs, about quarter to eleven, I was feeling fine. I felt well and lithe and beautiful. I felt grand, Ted was out in the garden, and the dining room was full of sunshine. I turned on the radio and a most enticing dance was playing. I felt so fine, so happy, so well, I began to dance. All alone by myself in the little room, I danced and danced. I danced every dance the band gave out. I was happy. Happy. Then, ten minutes after the band finished, came the first siren of the day, eleven fifty-five a.m. It lasted for an hour, and when the all clear came I was back to my normal sobriety. Four raids today.

- *MONDAY, SEPTEMBER 16, 1940* -

A day of incessant raids: six raids.

- *TUESDAY, SEPTEMBER 17, 1940* -

The second warning of the day sounded just now at nine ten a.m. The first lasted from eight to eight forty-five a.m. Last night was one of the very worst yet. When the all clear came just before three o'clock, we decided to go up to bed. We thought the Germans were through for the night. Not a bit of it! Just before four, the sirens sounded again, and the onslaught, lasting until five thirty-five a.m., was even heavier than in the first part of the night. The main attack, of course, was on London, but what damage was done we have not been told yet.

When Ted came in from mass, at eight this morning, he told me that one bomb hit the presbytery last night, but bounced off the roof again without doing much damage. The Germans deliberately pick out churches and hospitals for targets. They have hit Westminster Abbey, and nearly destroyed St. Paul's Cathedral. However, with the latter we were lucky. A bomb weighing a ton buried itself in Dean's Yard, by Amen Corner, but did not go off. At awful risk our demolition squad was able to dig it out and rush it to Hackney Marshes, and it exploded there. Had it exploded when it fell, the whole Cathedral would have been brought to the ground.

Buckingham Palace has been bombed three times. Hits have been made on the Law Courts, Trafalgar Square, the Houses of Parliament, and St. Thomas's Hospital. Cheapside is practically laid flat. Regent Street has suffered badly, and Victoria Station and Clapham Junction are practically wiped out. Nearly every London hospital has been bombed, and many churches. Some are quite demolished. Many city shelters, built to shelter hundreds of people, have been hit. On Sunday the R.A.F. brought down one hundred and eighty-five German machines, one hundred and thirty-five of them bombers. Our losses are supposed to be only twenty-five machines and twelve pilots. Maybe. Who really knows what the truth is? All we really know is what we actually see and suffer for ourselves.

As far as can be conjectured, this sort of war can go and is going on indefinitely. God help us all, it's simply hell on earth. Today is cloudy and windy. The equinox is near. Clouds are worse for us than clear skies, for the Germans can hide behind the clouds and bomb us before we know they are over us. Oh my God, what a world! Now the clock has struck ten and everything is quiet outside, though the all clear has not been given yet. Oh, here it comes, ten o'clock. Well, now I must bathe and get dressed before the next warning sounds. I have to cook this morning too.

Three more raids today.

- *WEDNESDAY, SEPTEMBER 18, 1940* -

Eight raids today. Eight warnings. This is the worse day yet. Last night was terrible. London is the main objective. Here in Romford, Victoria Road was hit for the second time; three stores and four houses demolished there. On Eastern Road, the Inland Revenue Offices were destroyed, and on South Street, Jays, the furniture shop. Again, the Germans must have been trying for the Railway Bridge and station, as all these places lay near it.

Mrs. Branney came in this morning, between raids, and Mrs. Jude came into lunch. Mrs. Jude had a tale that invasion has been tried. She says her window cleaner man, who came from Frinton yesterday, told her that at Frinton hundreds of dead Germans are being washed up on the shore. Maybe.

- *THURSDAY, SEPTEMBER 19, 1940* -

Three thirty p.m. Only one raid so far today. After a very long night raid, lasting from eight o'clock last night until half past five this morning, all has been quiet except for one short warning lasting from eight fifty-five a.m. until nine ten a.m. The night was awful. There is indiscriminate bombing against London. The BBC said the casualties were again very heavy; in central London over ninety known to be killed, and more than three hundred severely wounded. Oxford Street, Berwick Street, Berkley Square, Piccadilly, Grosvenor Square, Marble Arch, all got it last night. This is just plain murder.

When Ted came into lunch he told me he had had a mother and daughter in the office this morning, looking for a flat, and they told him they had been bombed three times! First in Poplar, where their house was demolished, then in Walthamstow, where they had gone for refuge, and again in a church, St. James the Great, where they had been transferred for safety.

One night last week, over three hundred men, women, and children were destroyed in a school, to which they had been taken 'for safety' after their homes had been destroyed. There is no safety in London anywhere. Hell! Hell! Goddamn Hitler.

I am most awfully tired, and getting very cranky. Nerves, of course. Last night Ted gave me a whiskey, but it didn't help me to sleep anyway. Ted rolls up on the floor and goes sound off, but I lay on the sofa and quake. Sometimes I can doze off in a lull, but directly the guns begin again, and I awake immediately. The barrage is very heavy, but the planes fly over steadily just the same. In daylight our men can bring them down, or chase them away, but at night it is a much more difficult job. Modern war. My God, it's awful.

I notice I'm not praying so much. Either I'm getting used to bombardment, or else I've got greater confidence in our A.A. guns.

Anyhow, my thoughts are straying again to Mrs. Eddy and her Christian Science. It is because I hate the works and words of men so much. I listen to the treacle that comes over the air—men talking—and I listen to Ted and his damn foolish chatter, and I know I hate the minds and talk of men. I hate men. I look at this world, which men have made, and I listen to their explanation and their exhortations, and I despise the idiots. Then they explain the almighty, and the mind and intentions of God! I think them presumptuous, silly fools, and I think their 'religion' worthless. No, give me a woman's religion. Give me a woman's reason. No woman can be such a damn fool as a damn fool man.

Why must God be masculine? Oh, Christian theologies all seem to me so childish. I listen to Ted, so naïve, but thinking he's so full of wisdom! I simply lump him for what he was in his beginnings, a Primitive Methodist. Well, that's all right for that type of mind, but it's not my type of mind, and I simply can't stomach it.

I notice that Ted never expects intelligence in his listeners, never expects even an ordinary standard of education. As for culture, all his assumptions are that it is non-existent.

As water seeks its own level, so do people. We are happiest when we are with our own kind, the sort of people we sprung from. So with Ted, he came from the poor and the uneducated, the chapelgoer's, and unconsciously he assumes that all people in the world are only those sorts of people. I find this dreary and boring. Ignorant people bore me. They may be good, they may be saints, but Lord, how they bore me!

Here is something, which interests me. It is a letter, which was printed in last Saturday's *Times*. I transcribe:

Sir, in my great misery, I came across the following by Sir Walter Raleigh, written in 1596. Hoping it may comfort others as it has me, I send it to you:

"I believe that sorrows are dangerous companions, converting bad into evil, and evil to worse, and do us no other service than multiply harms. They are the treasures of weak hearts and the foolish, the mind that entertained them is as the earth and dust whereon sorrows and adversities of the world do, as the beasts of the field, tread, trample and defile. The mind of man is that part of God, which is in us, which by how much it is subject to passion by so much it is further from Him that gave it to us. Sorrows draw not the dead to life but the living to death."

I am, Sir, the father of a missing pilot. St. James's Street. S.W.I.

Yes. The mind of man is that part of God which is in us.

My mind is that part of God which is in me: and my mind is all I have in this world to help me. Reason, Conscience, and Love, which Voysey used to preach about.

My mind. Without my mind, I am not. I cannot put my mind in blinkers. I cannot bamboozle my mind. I believe, as I must, not as I'm told. I cannot do otherwise. As a man thinketh in his heart, so he is. Ted is one sort of a man, and I'm another. I'm not masculine at all. I'm woman. I feel as a woman, and I think as a woman, no matter what the pundits lay down. I accept no man's values, no man's rulings, and no man's authorities. I know my own heart, my own mind, my own soul, and my own God. My God is not the old Jehovah, not the gentle Jesus. My God is the God that Jesus was talking about: Light, Life, Love,

Wisdom, Beauty, Spirit, Truth, Joy. The spirit of truth, the comforter; The father in me, and me in the father; The mind of God in my mind.

Oh well, I cannot stop to sort this out now, but it is like the bouquet Mrs. Eddy made up. I don't care if she was a plagiarist. In fact, I don't care what sort of woman she was. She did get a hold of a great idea, and she did get it over to the world, especially to the world of women, who needed and still need a woman to speak the mind of woman. Men have spoken for us too long. We will speak for ourselves now. At least, I'm jolly sure I will. There is no man living who can speak for me. No man can tell me anything contrary to my own mind and have me accept it. As for accepting the man! Oh, I groan.

- FRIDAY, SEPTEMBER 20, 1940 -

Eleven thirty a.m., air raid is on. The first warning of the day sounded at eleven ten. The weather is colder, cloudy, and blustery. The airplanes are passing and circling overhead, but I've heard no guns or bombs yet. Probably the main attack is again on the city. Last night was a most awful night. The warning was given at eight p.m. and our guns went into action immediately. The all clear did not sound until five fifty a.m. this morning. The BBC announced at eight that the damage on London had not been so sever as in some previous nights, most of the bombs falling on the outskirts of the city, in the East, Southeast, and Essex.

Right here in Romford, it was one of the most terrifying nights of the war. Bombs seemed to be falling all around us. I have not heard yet what damage was done, as nobody has been in yet. I was most horribly frightened and fell back again into my praying. This is instinctive and primitive. There is nothing else one can do but call upon God. Reason simply has nothing to do in such a situation of terror and helplessness.

Last night the Archbishop of York gave a talk on the air, "What is wrong with the world?" I like this man. He does talk sense. Sense, which is neither male nor female; sense, which is truth and reason. Why isn't there more churchman like him? Why isn't he made the chief spokesman for the Religion of England, instead of that old timeserving dodderer, the Archbishop of Canterbury?

Later in the evening, Thomson from next door came in. He wanted to telephone to Mrs. Thomson, in Cullompton. He told us that Plessis had been bombed on the previous night. They employ seven thousand people. Luckily, no one had been killed. He also told us of different experiences of various people in the firm, who live in the East End. Walthamstow has been particularly badly hit. In one 'rescue' school, three hundred and ninety-three people had been killed in one raid. He said that on Wednesday night, when the raids began again, the women of Walthamstow began screaming. The A.R.P. wardens had to remove them forcibly, "and their screaming was awful."

Of course it would be. The damned lying papers, and news reporters, and BBC announcers, will insist that the people are standing up to the raids with fortitude. "Grim and gay," says Churchill. I don't believe it. No woman can be gay about war. Women loathe war, and all war-makers. Women recognize the common sense of Jesus, who said, "Go and be reconciled with your adversary quickly, whilst you are yet in the way, and before he delivers you to the judge and you will be fined to your last penny." Women are not fools. Women are life preservers, never destroyers. Women know costs, and women will not, and cannot, waste.

There goes the all clear. I must go. I must cook a lunch, so Au-Revoir.

EPISODE #19

- SATURDAY, SEPTEMBER 21, 1940 -

We had only one other daytime raid yesterday. It lasted from seven fifty p.m. until eleven fifty-five p.m. So, when the all clear came, we went upstairs to bed. However, the warning came again at one twenty this morning, and lasted until half past five. This was an awful period, and I thought every minute we should be struck. There was one most awful explosion, which nearly frightened me to death.

When Ted came into breakfast, he was ready to weep. The big explosion we had heard had been a land mine, and it had exploded in Havering Drive. Amongst others, the Ryecroft house had been destroyed, and the whole family killed. Ted was grieving for young Peter Ryecroft, a young musician Ted liked very much. Bombs had been dropped in various spots; one at Strathmore opposite the laundry; two on Oakland's Avenue; one on Kingston Road, opposite the nursing home; one in the back brook at Arden Cottage; and one by the post office on Carlton Parade. Water and gas mains were broken, and we were without gas here until repairs were completed at about five this evening. Our other raids today were from eleven fifteen a.m. 'til eleven fifty a.m.; six ten until seven twenty p.m.' and the last given at eight eighteen p.m. is still proceeding.

It is worse and worse. Last night's raid lasted until four forty-five a.m. this morning. Another land mine was dropped, this time between Stanley Avenue and Carlton Road. About two hundred houses are shattered and down, but luckily nobody was killed!

Two more raids today. I am sick with fright and nerves. I keep crying. I long to be in America. If I had money, I would fly on The Clipper. As it is, I must stay here. Oh, God preserve us!

- MONDAY, SEPTEMBER 23, 1940 -

It was another awful night. Our last evening's raid began at seven ten p.m. but the all clear came at two forty-five a.m. Ted went up to bed but I didn't. I knew the Germans would be back again before daylight, and sure enough, back they came at three thirty a.m. Ted, of course, came downstairs, very promptly. The all clear came at six o'clock. On the seven o'clock news we were told of the sinking of one of the vessels carrying refugee children to Canada! The ship was torpedoed and sunk over six hundred miles out in the Atlantic last Tuesday night. The full ship's company totaled four hundred and six, including two hundred and fifteen of the crew and one hundred and ninety-one passengers, including the children. Only one hundred and twelve were rescued, and two hundred and ninety-four were drowned in all, thirteen children. Seven traveling under evacuation scheme were landed from the rescuing warship.

Ninety evacuee children were traveling with nine escorts. Only seven of these children and two of their escorts have been landed. The remaining eighty-three children and seven escorts have been lost.

This is German warfare, on par with the present indiscriminate bombing of the women and children of London. The whole civilized world curses Hitler. I hope he burns in Hell forever. Four thirty p.m. now. We have had two more raids for the day so far. It has been announced that the King will broadcast to the nation at six o'clock this evening. So I expect we shall get a heavy raid right then.

I went in to see Dr. Keighley this afternoon. I am still losing weight, but my leg is still very inflamed, and painful. She gave me some medicine for my nerves today. I am all on edge, broody and weepy. I feel I cannot endure this damn war any longer. I've got to endure it.

Mrs. Ryecroft was found in the debris of her house, but not the slightest trace of Peter could be found. Mrs. Ryecroft was pinned right through her breast by a big beam. The rescue squad had to saw her in half to extricate her body. This is horrible. I weep and weep. I think such violent and sudden death may descend on me in any hour, and I weep for my children, whom I may never see again. My boys. Oh God, preserve me, and give me my children in this world again.

When speaking of the Ryecroft's, Ted said, "But they are all in Heaven!" Such a remark drives me crazy. Heaven! What one wants is life in this world. Would it console me to think my dear ones were in Heaven? No, not ever. I want life here, where I know it, in the flesh. I want my sons to live their full human span, not to be destroyed in their flower. Oh God, save us, save us, and bring this war to a speedy end.

- *THURSDAY, OCTOBER 3, 1940* -

I am in an awful mood. I am sick with my leg, which gets no better. I am angry and miserable with this loathsome devilish war, and I am fed up with Ted. I feel I hate men and all their stupidities. I am sick to death of my particular man. I loathe marriage, and what I long for is not the freedom of Europe, but my freedom. Oh to be free! To have my life, and my body, to myself! Ted is intolerable to me. As time goes on, everything that is primitive Methodist and working class in his origins, comes more and more to the front; and this is the kind of person that is not my kind of person, never was and never will be.

There was another interruption and annoyance. My neighbor, Mrs. Thomson, called in and has only just left. She comes in every time there is a warning, and this is just too much of a good thing. She is a nice enough person all right, but another that is not my sort, so I get bored with her and her chatter. I would rather be alone. However, since she doesn't like to be alone in an air raid, I don't choke her off. I would let anybody in during a raid; it is so awful to be frightened. Yesterday we had nine warnings! We have had no warning yet this morning, but Mrs. Thomson has been in to see me anyhow.

A week or two back during a raid Selma went to Arden Cottage, and her father wouldn't let her in the house. He stood in the doorway and prevented her entering. He swore at her, and told her to go back to her own place. That's Bert Thompson; dirty selfish old beast. I would let anybody into my house if a raid were on; gypsy or tramp, or any friend or stranger that asked shelter; but old Bert refuses admittance to his own daughter. Yes, Selma's a fool, but she is still his own flesh and blood. He begot her. I say damn the Thompsons. I think they are the coldest blooded and self-willed lot I have ever come near. They are egoists, and without natural affections.

Ted is on my nerves most frightfully. As for his religion, he's worse than ever. Every morning he will go to mass. The all clear does not sound now 'til half past five or six o'clock. Any sensible person would then go to sleep, safe quiet sound sleep, for an hour or an hour and a half and allow the other members of a house to sleep too. Not Ted. Oh dear no! He must dress and go to church, and he wants his breakfast early, please. What sense, what religion, what goodness, is there in that? We haven't slept upstairs in bed for five weeks or more. I sleep, as much as I can, on the sofa, pushed over into a corner, and Ted lies on the floor on cushions under the dining table, and all night long the guns go and the bombs drop. You would think that when dawn came and an hour of quietness, a man would sleep, wouldn't you? Yes, and a man would. Not Ted! Not my pious idiot. He has to dress and go to mass. He also has to do whatever else he wants to do. He wants what he wants when he wants it. When he wants it. He calls that love. Well I don't. I call that unadulterated selfishness. He doesn't love me because he *loves* me. He takes me because he loves himself. He wants a physical satisfaction, and because I am his wife, he just takes it for granted. That isn't love. Oh no. It's just gross beastliness.

Last night he wanted, and I put him off. I have no feeling. I am angry and miserable and frightened by the war. My leg makes me feel sick with pain and I am very uncomfortable, only partially undressed and huddled on a couch. Well, he retired to his pillows on the floor, but in the early morning, an hour before the all clear came, he was at me again. I simply couldn't. I feel I should cry. So then he wanted to argue the situation! This only made me stonier and angrier than ever.

Ted and his damned talk! Oh, I am so sick of it! Ted's superciliousness, his belittling, his sneering, his criticizing are wearing me down. His damned tongue! So he left me, in a huff, and went and dressed himself, and then he sat and read Sir Walter Scott until it was time to go to church. That's it, the damned church! If I had given in to him, he would have dressed and gone out to early church just the same. Oh. I knew that quite well. That's what I can't stand. I can't mix up love and religion. I can't reconcile the two, not ever. What I want is love. "Let him kiss me with the kisses of his mouth." Yes, let him. That is not Ted's way. If he ever kissed me, called me by a pet name, spoke endearingly, fondled me, coaxed me, brought me a tiny gift, showed me even ordinary affection and comradeship, but no. So I freeze.

I have even stopped wanting this sort of love and these signs of love. I only want to get away from him, not to have to see him more, not to have to listen to him more, not to have to talk to him, because whatever I say is wrong. He will correct my grammar or phrasing if he cannot correct my reason or sentiment. Above all, to be able to forget him. What I want is my own life; myself for myself. To be free of him, Oh God, to be free! Marriage lasts too long. I've known that for years.

Two forty-five p.m. and it is raining heavily, and no warnings today, so far, though I have heard guns several times. Feeling better for my dinner. We had hot roast loin lamb, potatoes, and vegetable marrow, stewed pears, flapjacks and coffee. Here is again one of my nuisances. I have to cook a midday dinner every day, and so I never have a clear day to myself. I have no time. Very literally, I have no time. This again is one of the reasons Ted and I are at odds so much. We see too much of each other, and he is around the house entirely too much, considering the sort of man he is. For Ted is a petty man. He is also a bossy man, so he interferes with things that are none of his business, and petty things, like how many slices of bread I cut, or where I place a chair, or open a window, or a stove-draught. He wants to know what is in a bureau drawer, and tells me the kettle is boiling. And so on. I don't say anything, but I chafe. He keeps tabs on the pantry and watches supplies. This is because he is wasting himself. He is applying to a tiny private home the energies and qualities he should be using on a big business. I find it very trying.

He told me lately I was a damned bad housekeeper and I ought to be ashamed of myself. This is because I threw away half a loaf, which had begun to go moldy. He didn't make me cross. I just thought how silly he was. I never did set up to be a perfect housekeeper, and I have done an awful lot of housekeeping in thirty-five years. Anyhow, I didn't marry him to be his housekeeper. If he doesn't like my housekeeping, he must lump it. Again, I know from where this source of criticism derives: from Herbert. If Ted and I see too much of each other, it is equally true that Ted sees too much of Herbert. Herbert is an uncouth, ignorant, brutal, selfish old bully. Herbert holds the Victorian working man's ideas about women and about wives. That's why Dorothy couldn't stand him. To Herbert a wife is a servant and a possession, a creature that exists primarily to minister to her owner, and moreover, she should be thankful to him that he supports her.

That's what I feel about Ted and his "love." As he takes a smoke or a drink whenever he feels like it, so also he takes a wife; she is to be handy to him, like a bread box or a cold joint or a whiskey bottle, for when he happens to have an appetite. I loathe such love. I loathe such takings. As for his religion, I loathe that too. Ted places his religion before everything else in the world, certainly before live flesh and blood.

- *FRIDAY, OCTOBER 4, 1940* -

Yesterday I was interrupted by the noise of large explosions and a sudden warning. Mrs. Thomson came rushing in, in a panic, and was followed soon after by Mrs. Jude, very pale and very frightened. She had been walking on South Street when everything happened in a clap, and she had to run all the way up to this house. It is not safe to be on the streets now after any warning, for the Germans have taken to low diving, and then machine-gunning anyone in sight. They gun trains and buses, people in the streets, workers on the roads and fields, and even the cattle and sheep in the meadows.

This particular warning lasted until five p.m., soon after which Ted came into his tea. Mrs. Thomson was still here, but Mrs. Jude had left, because of being home for Mary Bernadette. Then Ted was rude to Mrs. Thomson, at some remark she made. He led her on and then put her through the third degree with questioning. It is Ted's delight to make the other person look like a fool. He thinks he is smart. Really he is colossally rude. Besides, who commissioned him to correct everybody? By what infallible standard of general wisdom? Ted is fatuously presumptuous, and as I listen to him I think he is a damned fool. Like this morning at breakfast he was telling me about a man in the office yesterday who got so cross. He had sent the man to look at a house, and on his return to the office the man asked, "What about the roof?" and "What about the crater?"

"So I said, 'well, what about the crater?'

"The man said, 'Yes, that's what I'm asking you, what about the crater?'

"So I said again, 'well, what about it? You know more about it than I do. I haven't seen it; you've just been there.'

"And he got so cross and went out."

Ted laughed. He thought that was funny. I don't think that funny at all, or the way to do business. It seems as though Ted can't be polite; if he didn't know there was a crater before the door, he could surely have civilly told his inquirer he didn't know anything about it. Ted often tells me tales about how he scores off the people who come down into the office, and when they get cross, he is only amused. When they leave the office, as this man did yesterday, and as I have been told of others doing, Ted thinks they are wrong, not himself. It is a mania with him, correcting other people. It seems nobody answers him as he thinks they ought to answer him, and he will accept nobody's statement about anything. He is really peculiar about this, and he gets worse.

Last night the Germans were around here for a long time. The explosion of bombs about a quarter to one wakened me. There were so many of them, I lost count. It sounded as though they were trying for the station or the hospital again, and they came nearer, almost directly overhead, and the house shook. I expected to be blown up any minute. Ted slept through it all!

That racket died down, but there was another attack, nearly as bad, soon after three o'clock. Finally everything quieted, and at last I fell asleep, and I slept so soundly I did not hear the morning's all clear, nor wake up until Ted turned on the radio for the seven o'clock news. He remarked on my sleeping so soundly, but when I told him of the very bad night Romford had gone through, he said, "Are you sure you weren't dreaming?" I said no more. What is the use of talking to him? He went out to church, whistling.

As a matter of fact, last night was one of the worst we have had for over a week. I lay trembling, and could not hold still. I expected the house to be bombed any minute. I prayed without ceasing, but I prayed to God. Only God. *No* thought whatsoever of Jesus, or Mary, or Michael, or Joseph, came to my mind. Only God. Only God.

When the immediate danger receded, what I thought about was this book. I thought I might be killed any day or any night now. This book may be destroyed too if these premises are destroyed; or it may not be destroyed, it may be found and read. What if it is read? These outbursts about Ted, which I pen, aren't they unkind?

Yes, maybe they are unkind. Maybe I shouldn't put them down, maybe I should myself destroy them and quickly.

Do I want Ted to find out what I think about him? I feel about him? I wonder. Isn't he as tired of me as I am tired of him? Isn't it true we would both be happier apart?

Am I ashamed of what I have written? No, I am not ashamed. I try to state the truth. I try to find the truth of things for myself; that is, as they matter for myself. I am not a happy woman. I could have been a happy woman. I just happened to have married the wrong man, a very common tragedy. Ted is to me as I have described him to be. I am as I am, as this book must disclose, no matter what I try to disclose or to hide. So, let the record stand.

Five fifteen p.m. A warning was sounded at one o'clock, and the all clear has not been given yet. Mrs. Thomson has just left, as she must go cook a dinner for her husband. She has been here all afternoon. Ted came in at one fifteen p.m., said he was going to have his dinner, and anyhow, there was not many people in the shelter, as it was dinner hour. I remarked it was St. Francis Day, and he replied, "Yes, and *our* St. Francis too, old Bert's birthday today."

"How old today?"

"Seventy-two."

Not much of a saint in Bert's makeup. Ted is the saint of the Thompson family. Bert is a gross and sensual old beast. Ted said that benediction was at six tonight, so he would work late at the office, and go straight to benediction before coming home. So tea would be late tonight.

Now I must put this book away for the weekend. I would like to keep on writing; there is much I need to clear out of my system. However, there is no time. Mrs. Thomson has eaten my afternoon.

Every now and again we hear gunfire, but no planes overhead. Romford was not bombed last night. The noises I heard must have been in Dagenham, where Brigg's was bombed, and a school. There is a heavy impenetrable cloud overhead, and this is very dangerous, for the enemy cannot be seen. What will he do to us tonight, I wonder. Ilford got it badly yesterday afternoon, also Harold Park and Dagenham. In Harold Park a bomber dived and machine-gunned women on the street.

At eleven o'clock this morning Hitler and Mussolini met at Brenner Pass. What deviltry have they cooked up for the world today? Men! All Europe is being crucified for the ambitious policies of these two maniacs. Why do their own people submit to them? For they destroy their own as well as others. Why does the pope say nothing? Because he is an Italian? Or because he is just playing safe, saving his skin and his properties, like the rest of the plutocrats? Anyhow, he says nothing, no more than he did when Italy murdered Abyssinia, or raped Albania. I guess he is just another politician.

Well Au-Revoir. I have written enough for a while; too much, most likely.

EPISODE #20

- SUNDAY, OCTOBER 6, 1940 -

Seven fifty a.m. I open this book at this hour to cool my anger. We have just passed through a most awful night. The warning was given at seven thirty-five last night and the all clear did not come until six fifteen this morning. The guns opened up immediately on the warning, and have not ceased all night. It was the worst evening we have ever had. It was pretty bad Friday evening; so bad, that both Mr. and Mrs. Thomson came in here 'for company'. But about one o'clock this morning the raiders were directly overhead and began dropping bombs. I don't know yet where they fell, but one was so close that this house tottered. I began to cry. I couldn't help myself, in fact, I weep now, recording it. Ted was undismayed. There is callousness and cold-bloodedness about Ted, which I abhor. Well, at ten to seven he started to dress. At seven, the first warning of this day was given, but Ted proceeded with his dressing, and went to church in his usual way. He left the house at seven twenty though mass doesn't begin 'til eight, and he will not be back until nine twenty.

I feel furious with him. I say Ted Thompson is a maniac. I say his daily church going is an obsessive habit. I say his craving for communion is on par with a drunk's craving for alcohol. I say his self-given mania for correcting and instructing every person he comes in contact with is colossal impertinence, and I say none of his church going, none of his talking theology, none of his acts of piety is real religion or real goodness. I say it is all excessive unbearable self-righteousness and self-love in the nth degree.

Ted is a fool out and out. He didn't have to go to early church today. There is a mass at nine thirty and there is another mass at eleven a.m. Wouldn't any sensible man have taken two or three hours sleep this morning and allowed his household to sleep? Of course he would. Not Ted. This compulsion on him to go to early mass is maniacal. He is a maniac. Isn't it because of his craziness that we are here in England at all? That the twins are in the war? That Cuthie is a prisoner? Oh my God how I fret and fret for my children! In nights like this one, which we have just passed through, I fear I shall never see my children again. The bombs strike anywhere. They are just as likely to fall on this house as any other.

I think of Harold, of Eddie, of all of them, and my heart breaks with grief and longing. Ted? It is just as though he never had children at all. He moves along serene and blithe in his own world of dreams. He thinks of no one except the figures of this mythical world of Roman Catholicism. Like the old fool Petain, a Vichy, he is convinced that all the troubles of the world would be cured by the return of the people en mass to the church. That's all that matters to Ted, the church. He has no affection for anybody. Human beings do not matter to Ted except himself and his will and his own soul. That is all he can 'love'; his own soul. I say, curse him. He is an intolerable man, and I am impatient with this fool and so angry. Impatience and anger doesn't help any. Well, let me dress. Here is another day to get through.

Five thirty p.m. A few minutes ago Ted left the house to go to church. This is for the third time today. He is playing the organ, as Miss Hale is away.

A warning is still in progress, and only fifteen minutes ago the big gun was firing. The warning was given at two twenty p.m. and the barrage has been constant ever since. A whistling bomb fell very near, about four o'clock. Ted has gone out to church all the same. This is already our sixth warning for the day. How many people will be at church? The night's bombs fell in Slewins Lane.

- *MONDAY, OCTOBER 7, 1940* -

It is eight forty a.m. and another early writing. Ted left ten minutes ago for his Monday's round, and a warning is still on. It went at six forty-five a.m. and is the second one for today. After practically continuous raiding all yesterday, there was no warning given after the all clear at eight forty p.m., so we have had a quiet night, and the BBC says it has been the same all over England. This is the first raidless night since the intensive war on Great Britain began. It was a stormy night, wind and rain of the Equinox, but peace from the Germans.

Ted went upstairs to bed, and remained there 'til the warning at five fifty a.m., but I stayed down here on the couch and was at ease. Not to have Ted in the same room with me, that is a certain sort of bliss. I realized it when I lay down alone in the darkness that I was free from him, free from the constraint of his presence. For me to be with Ted is always to be under a sense of constraint. It has been that way from the beginning. He oppresses my spirit. From the very first weeks of our marriage it was like that. When he began to deride the things I cared about, when he began to maul at my inner woman, my personality, then I had to begin to protect myself, my secret self. It has always been like that; everything that is precious to me, and in me, I must hide, must protect. So it is a strain, a long strain. I do not hate him, but I long to be free of him, just to be free, forever free.

In our American life I did have long free days to myself; business and traveling took him away from the house on twelve hour stretches, but here in England I hardly ever have longer than a four hour period free from him, and in these short periods I have to get through my house jobs and listen to the neighborhood women, whom I cannot escape. That is why I cannot read or write or study anymore. I have no free time; house and husband and neighbors consume it all.

Now the war takes even more time away. It is impossible to do anything while the raids are on. All one can do is sit still in shelter, perhaps knit, perhaps pray, perhaps talk with someone who happens in, and drink tea or smoke a cigarette together. Most of the raids last at least an hour, and we get five or six a day. Last Wednesday we had nine. Then in-between raids we have to do our work. Then there are meals to fix, the everlasting meals. I am sick. My leg is really very bad. Often when the big guns go, often without warning, I feel a fissure in my leg crack. It seems as though this leg will never heal. The pain of it often makes me sick to my stomach. Sometimes I am even reduced to crying with the pain. I must go now and dress my leg, and this is a job, which takes me nearly an hour every day. Then I must bathe and dress, for I am still in my nightclothes. So Au-Revoir. Perhaps I can write again today. Writing, even the mere physical act, is my dope.

Ten fifteen a.m. and the first all clear of the day has just sounded. The first warning was given at eight forty. The all clear for the night did not come until seven this morning. Last night was the longest night of raids we have yet had. It began at seven forty p.m. I suppose as the longer nights increase we shall endure ever longer and longer hours of raiding. Sunday night was free of raids, but last night was worse than ever. Yesterday we were raided practically continuously. Saturday night's bombs fell on Stanley Avenue, the second time on Lodge Avenue, which is very close to us, and on Gideon Park. On Sunday afternoon they fell on the railway line, at Brentwood, and at Gidea Park, completely demolishing Gidea Park Station.

Today is a beautiful day, and in myself I feel very much better. Last night I was able to surrender to Ted for a little while (love on a sofa!), so my nerves are assuaged. My mind is not altered. My thoughts about we two are the same as ever. I have brought down a Dorothy Richardson to browse in; also Mrs. Eddy. I need these two good feminists to buck me up. When I listen to the drivel that men talk, in the house and on the radio, I scorn the whole darn shooting match of them. When I turned on for the eight o'clock news this morning there was an unctuous parson's voice saying, "In quietness and confidence shall ye possess your peace." Yes, exactly. What a tag to hand out to the world today! There is no quietness. There is no confidence. A hellish war is on, and there is no certainty that we are going to win it. For a whole year Hitler has been conquering Europe, and quite possibly he may conquer England too. It certainly looks that way. The strong-minded can possess their minds, true, but they cannot alter circumstances. The people who were bombed last night, the thousands who came up from a night in the Tubes this morning, in what quietness and confidence do they possess their peace?

Ten forty, second warning sounding, so Au-Revoir.

Two fifty p.m. As I knew it would happen, Mrs. Thomson was at my door before I could put this book away, and she stayed here through three warnings, until Ted came home for dinner. This is what I hate, this loss of my precious time. I want to be writing. I want to put down for my children the story of my life, my life as I see it and interpret it, and this desire is urging me more and more imperatively. When life for all of us in this island is becoming daily more dangerous and more precarious, I feel I must write now, whilst I know I still have time in the land of the living. Not that it would matter if my children never knew the truth of my life. At the back of everything I suppose is my deep desire to stat the truth of myself, ready to await the recognition of that female descendant of myself who will be most like me; a repetition of myself. This is great egotism, of course, and I know it. There it is.

Fifty or sixty years hence, some other woman, some lonesome creature of my blood may be able to find in my old writings the explanations for her own cursed self. All I can manage are these sporadic diaries. What I want to do is to write the whole story from the beginning, in one connected, straightforward whole. Because of the daily conditions of existence, this I cannot do. It is a pity because I feel my powers failing. If I could have uninterrupted time, no housework, no neighbors, no air raids, no routines, I could write. I could write very well, and I know it. As things are I can do very little, practically nothing. My days are frittered away, and I with them. Henley wrote, "I am the master of my Fate." But Henley was a man.

Chamberlain Resigns; Churchill Elected

Last night again we had a little love on the sofa. This surprised me and was very pleasant. If only Ted could love me more and the church less we should get along together much better than we do. When I woke this morning, I was full of thoughts of Grandma Side. Perhaps I had been dreaming about her, though I do not recollect a dream. Perhaps it was because she stirs in my memory as a good feminist, the first I ever knew, and most likely the last I shall forget. Anyhow, I loved Grandma Side, and never forget her. If only a granddaughter of mine could know and understand and love me, as I know and understand and loved her. I should know content in my old age. Queer, isn't it? That two old people inhabit my mind in abiding affection for all my life? Grandma Side and Charles Voysey; over and over again throughout my years these two come to my mind.

We were full of visitors today. Myrtle Arch was here this morning, also Mrs. Thomson and, this afternoon, Mrs. Branney. Yesterday afternoon I had a long visit from Dick Brazier.

Raids have been very bad all day; six on London, but only three here in Romford, though the afternoon one lasted a long time, from two forty-two p.m. until four twenty p.m.

- THURSDAY, OCTOBER 10, 1940 -

Eleven ten a.m. Mrs. Thomson only recently left. We have had two bad raids already this morning. The first one, between nine and ten this morning, we had swarms of machines overhead, beyond counting. Our men took off towards the river, and the Germans, in droves, came sweeping in from behind. Flying right over these houses. No bombs dropped, the battle must have been elsewhere.

Last night was a terrible night. I don't know how we can keep on enduring these nights. Bombs dropped on North Street and in the stadium on the London Road. No casualties! I'm beyond praying. I just lay and shake and cry. Churchill makes his famous speeches, but Hitler is winning the war anyhow, no matter what they say. If it lay with women, we should call for an armistice tomorrow. What sense is there in this stupid fighting? No! Men talk themselves into a war, and then they talk themselves into going on with it. Men's talk, how I hate men's talk, men's minds! Though I'll make an exception for the Archbishop of York! He talks on the air once a week now, and most of what he says makes sense. "He talks like a Catholic," says Ted.

He doesn't. He talks like a man of sense and a gentleman. He is the cultured Christian, speaking to sensible people.

By the way, here is a delicious tidbit that I must chronicle. It came over the radio this morning. The early morning parson was talking about the humility of Jesus, and he gave this anecdote. "It is told of Saint Philip Neri," he said (and what's an Anglican got to do with St. Philip Neri?), "that he was sent on a mission by the Pope to inquire into the sanctity and credentials of a certain nun in Rome who was making a stir with the populace with her good deeds and prophecies. The people were saying she was a saint. So Saint Philip Neri was sent to make investigations concerning her. After a long journey he arrived at her convent, all travel-stained and weary. Without waiting to tidy himself from his journey, he went to the convent as he was and asked for the nun. He was shown into the parlor, and she came to him at once. Thereupon, sitting in his chair, he stretched out his leg and asked the nun to take off his muddy boots for him. The nun indignantly refused to do so. So this was enough for St. Phillip. He left the convent at once and went straight to the Pope. He reported to the Pope, 'You have nothing to fear from that woman. She has true humility'."

Beautiful story, isn't it? Such a man's story, all the masculine point of view. Just showing what men expect from women, service and obedience, and the acceptance, without the slightest demur, of man's orders and man's discourtesies. Who the hell was St. Phillip Neri to request a woman to take his muddy boots off! Moreover, this must have been a woman of learning, as well as of great repute. But no! The female must grovel to the male!

This morning's parson hands it out as an edifying story. Lord! What fools men are!

Eleven forty a.m. The Sainsbury boy has just been in with the groceries. He tells me that four bombs were dropped in the first raid this morning. One got "The Crown" and nearby houses on the London Road; one fell in a field in the Arterial Road; and two fell on Marlborough Road, destroying several houses and two cars that were on the road. The men in the cars were killed; one had his head blown off. One of the houses was the home of Sainsbury's porter, who, the boy says, has been released to go home.

Two of Sainsbury's men were killed on the street in that bad raid we had on a midday in August. Oh God! This fool war!

EPISODE #21

- FRIDAY, OCTOBER 11, 1940 -

The war is getting worse and worse. On Wednesday night the Germans bombed forty districts of London. Last night they bombed thirty-six districts. Our fifth warning for today is just sounding. Last night we had an awful fright, soon after eight o'clock. The alarm had been sounded at seven twenty-five. Soon after eight we heard a bomb whistling, descending. We thought surely it was going to hit this house. Ted ducked and got under the table! There were two close following thirds, the house rocked, but we were not hit. Then two more followed, a little further off. Altogether Romford received nine. I sat and cried. I cannot pray anymore. I seem just paralyzed.

The firing went on the rest of the night, but no more hits came in this neighborhood. Today we learnt that the evening's bombs hit in Victoria Road (for the fourth time!), Albert Road, Lodge Avenue, and Westmoreland Avenue. Craters made and houses demolished, including two pubs, but no casualties.

Our first alarm sounded this morning at seven thirty-five whilst Ted was at church. Mrs. Thomson came in at once, and stayed for breakfast. Ted left early for the office, but before Mrs. Thomson left the second warning sounded, at eight fifty a.m. The raid lasted for one hour.

The third was at ten forty-five a.m. until twelve fifty p.m., during which time Mr. Kessey was here; the fourth at two thirty p.m. until three twenty p.m.

It is impossible to get anything done, and the wear and tear on our nerves is exhausting. If only I had some money, I would board The Clipper and fly to New York. I was only saying to Ted last night, just before the bombs fell, how awful these nights were, and I didn't know how I was going to stand a whole winter of them. A dozen nights like these last two nights and I'm afraid I shall go raving mad. The men are still talking war, war, and war. The politicians infuriate me. Anyhow, they don't fight. They only specify and egg wars on.

- *SATURDAY, OCTOBER 12, 1940* -

Today the Thomson's called in at the office and gave a week's notice. Mrs. Thomson is going to Devon, and he is going to share a house with a fellow worker at Plessis whose wife and children have gone to Bradford, and who lives in Ilford. So it is goodbye Mrs. Thomson. Both of them spent the evening in here, and it was as well they did, for in chatting and laughing together we were distracted from the outside noises.

- *SUNDAY, OCTOBER 13, 1940* -

After all, it is not goodbye Mrs. Thomson! She came in here about noon, all tears, to say she had changed her mind. She could see, she said, that John really didn't want her to go, so she couldn't leave him. He had gone down to the station, to see could he get his money back on the R-ticket, which he had bought yesterday. All morning they had been packing up, and now, the work was in vain, and everything to be unpacked again. So I invited them to dinner. I knew they had no supplies in their house. After dinner, when they returned next door to work whilst there was still daylight, I invited them to come back for tea, at blackout time. Of course they came, and in a very happy and united frame of mind together. After tea we played bridge for a couple of hours. During the evening the uproar picked up again outside, worse than ever.

The moon is now coming to the full, as there is plenty of light for the raiders. In the middle of the evening they were right overhead, and we heard bombs dropping very nearby. The explosions were terrific. One whistling bomb sounded as though it was going to drop at our very door. I felt we ought to duck under the table. We didn't. We went right on playing bridge. The men didn't budge, just winked at each other. This was just as well for us; they steadied us.

This is the anniversary of Arthur's birthday. Arthur always thought luck was against him. Anyhow, he's safely out of this bloody mess of a world. He would have been a man in his fifties now, with a son to be sucked into this damnable, horrible, crazy war.

- MONDAY, OCTOBER 14, 1940 -

It is three fifty p.m., just back from the doctor's in time to get under cover from the raiding. Raids have been going on all morning. An all clear did not sound until two twelve, so I've just had time to get my visit in.

At last I am on the mend. My leg is healing. I am to keep on with the white ointment for another week, and then when she sees the leg next week she will decide whether or not I can put it back into its usual plaster of viscopaste. During this week I have lost three and a quarter pounds, which is very encouraging, nearly a half-pound a day. Last week I didn't lose an ounce. If I could get down to thirteen stone I would be satisfied. After all, I am a very tall woman.

Mrs. Jude was in to see me this morning. As usual, she gave me the town news. She only just got into the house before the warning sounded, at about half past eleven, and all the time she was here, a battle was going on above us. Ten bombs were dropped in Romford last night. The most serious damage was in North Street, where Haysom's was struck and completely demolished. Haysom's is Romford's largest furniture store, and occupied nearly a block. This morning there is nothing there but rubble and cinders. No lives lost. Sunday, of course, and not a soul was on the premises. Presumably the Jerry's were trying for the Romford food storage plant, which is just behind Haysom's. North Street and the Arterial Road frequently get hit. The Arterial Road, of course, is a military road, so a legitimate target. It has trenches all along it, with soldiers cap-a-pie, and big gun emplacements, and tank traps, and so on. The funny thing is, the soldier's, or the trenches, never get hit, only the neighboring shops and houses.

- WEDNESDAY, OCTOBER 23, 1940 -

I have something marvelous to record. We had an almost quiet night last night. The alert sounded at six fifty-five p.m. and the all clear, after a noisy evening, sounded at eleven-thirty p.m. Then we only had one short period of danger in the night, from about twelve thirty a.m. to two a.m. All day we had no warnings until now, the first one sounding at six thirty-five p.m. This is probably for the night. The weather has been bad, that's why we've had practically twenty-four hours peace. It's too foggy for flying. There have been sporadic raiders today, but not in this neighborhood. Yesterday, Laval saw Hitler in Paris. The rumor now is that France is going to declare war on England. Well, maybe! Anything is possible in this crazy lunatic war.

- *FRIDAY, OCTOBER 25, 1940* -

Two months today to Christmas, as Ted remarked at breakfast.

It is ten thirty a.m. and a raid on. After several days of cold mist and rain, today is a beautiful day; therefore the raids have begun early. The first warning went at eight fifty this morning, and there is no clearance. Twice already I've had to go into my corner and grab a cushion for my head at the threatening whistles very near and overhead. This makes me furious. I am so angry at this war. The stupidity of it, even more than the cruelty and fearfulness, fills me with rage. Men, blasted fool men, creating war. When I listen to all the poppycock that's spoken on the air, I'm simply derisive. For here are men again, exhorting, bragging, and begging, diddling with facts, and trickling out sob-stuff about glory and about self-sacrifice. Damn lot of plausible Pharisees, that's what most of the talking men are. Who are they? The old men.

It's the young ones, the ignorant, innocent, inexperienced boys, who are sent out to die. Some smarmy parson on the war this morning was talking about the acceptance of pain and suffering; the same old lines, the same glibness and triteness. I say suffering does not ennoble. There aging is a man's word: noble. I ask, why must suffering be accepted as the will of God? I should say that 90% of the suffering in the world is not the will of God, but the infliction by men upon mankind and it need not be.

Two fifty p.m. Mrs. Cavus came calling and stayed until dinnertime. She looked very pretty in a new winter outfit, brown in color, and chic. Of course we talked about the war, and agreed together that if the women could have any say in the matter, it would end tomorrow.

At one o'clock news we heard that Petain had seen Hitler, last night. Hitler also saw Franco yesterday. What are they cooking up for Europe now? Petain is eighty-four, and a pious Catholic. He was the man who surrendered France to Hitler. Now he talks about the salvation of France laying in her return to an agricultural economy, the cessation of the practice of birth control, the destruction of Masonry, and a return to the bosom of the Catholic Church. If only all men would return to the true faith, which, of course, is Roman Catholicism, then everything in the world would be lovely. Silly old fool! Old, that's what's the matter with him. What about the Pope? The Pope says nothing, and keeps on saying nothing. Mussolini makes the Italians behave disgracefully, but the Pope never utters even one little admonition. No. The Pope is an Italian, and a politician, and he plays for safety. The Italians marched into Albania on a Good Friday, and the Pope even said nothing to that.

There used to be a question when I was young: What would Jesus do? Anyhow, Jesus didn't sit in a palace, with armed guards, and keep a shut mouth whilst his countrymen behaved like skunks. After all, when one stops to think about which are the Catholic countries, which the Catholic people, who would choose to be a Catholic? Ireland, the dirty Irish, the quarrelsome, murdering, lying Irish; Spain, with the Spaniards making murderous civil war; Belgium, with the Belgian coarseness and their Judas

King; France, with Frenchmen so cynical or so soppy; Mexico with its illiterate and murderous Mexicans; and Italy, with its rape of Abyssinia, annexation of Albania, its stab in the back at falling France, the treacherous Italians. No, a white man has no sort of affiliation with any one of them. Oh, what moment of madness when I joined the church!

- SUNDAY, OCTOBER 27, 1940 -

It is a rotten day. Ted very teasing, and air raids galore. Today is Grandma Side's birthday.

- MONDAY, OCTOBER 28, 1940 -

The Italians have declared war on Greece. An ultimatum was handed to the Greeks at three a.m. this morning, to which a favorable answer was demanded by six a.m. The Greeks refused to accede to the Italian demands, so at six o'clock the Italians began their attack on Greece. At seven o'clock the first air raid warning was sounded over Athens. Last night Hitler and Mussolini met in Florence. I suppose this further aggression was what they then decided upon. The filthy little Italians! What is the Pope going to say to them now? Is he going to say the same old nothing?

- MONDAY, NOVEMBER 4, 1940 -

Eleven a.m. for the first time in fifty-six nights we had no 'alert' last night. It is presumed that the heavy rain made the enemy's bases on the other side of the channel unsuitable for safe landing. Our first alarm for today sounded at ten a.m., and no all clear has come yet.

I have just finished bathing and dressing for the day, and I have had a very agreeable surprise. I decided to wear the black dress Miss Canham made for me about a year ago, and which I have never yet worn. It is miles too big! I have lost so much girth in my middle, the skirt now drops right to the ground. As it is, the dress is not wearable. I will keep it on for today so that Dr. Keighley can see for herself how I have diminished under her regime. I shall probably sign off with her today. Last Monday she told me to try my leg in viscopaste again, so on Thursday I put on fresh plasters, and to my great satisfaction, the leg has been quite comfortable under the plaster all week. So it would seem extravagant to visit her once a week simply to get weighed. I can continue to observe the diet she gave me, and reduce weight, without needing to pay her to step on her weighing machine. I have lost about thirty pounds since the beginning of August. My average loss is about two pounds per week. If I could get myself down to twelve stone, or somewhere around one hundred and seventy pounds, I shall be content to stay at that. After all, I am a very tall woman, and I do not want to look gaunt.

Well, with a new book, here is a new resolution. Or, rather, an old resolution reaffirmed. I made it this morning, and this is why. These last two or three weeks Ted has begun to read through all the Scott we have in the house. He has also gone around talking in what, I suppose, he thinks is an imitation of the Scottish accent and dialect. I haven't found it a bit amusing. It's so silly. It's typical of Ted, both the reading, and what he thinks is a joke, in his imitating. To me it is simply on par with the mind of a schoolboy of fourteen. Scott belongs to the schoolroom: and as for imitations, well they're childish, too. Last night Ted finished *The Heart of Midlothian*, whose heroine is that horrible girl, Jeannie Deans. At breakfast this morning he remarked, "Now I've finished Jeanie Deans."

"So you've lost an interest in life," I commented.

"Oh no. There are plenty of more Scotts to read. Anyhow I don't think this is one of his best, not enough story in it. Not enough action. He could have made a better story of it, I think."

"I never find much story in Scott. Take *The Bride of Lammermoor*, for instance. It's very dull. You plough on and you plough on and you plough on and nothing happens."

"Your language! You don't plough on. Why don't you express yourself correctly? What you mean is that the story is very inadequate and you don't like it. Isn't that it? Why you can't say what you mean, I don't know! 'Plough on and plough on'. Psh"

He kept on about 'ploughing on', etc. etc., for another five minutes. I said no more. I didn't answer his questions as to why I spoke as I did, or speak as I do. I said nothing. Inside I took a vow. I vow that beyond the necessities of courteous speech required by etiquette in the routine of daily life, I will never speak to Ted Thompson, or in front of him, again. To speak spontaneously, or to express any private opinion in front of Ted, is to be corrected or derided, and squashed. Always squashed. Who the hell is he to correct everybody's utterance? Only one day last week he came home mightily pleased with himself, and told me a tale about how he had corrected somebody in the shelter. I've forgotten the incident he related, but he wound up by saying, "I didn't half make him look a fool, I can tell you. I put him in his place all right. He did look an ass when I'd finished with him!"

He was so pleased with himself; he'd been scoring over a stranger. Why? Isn't it horrible? Yes, conversation with Ted is impossible. Well, I won't talk to him, or to anyone else when he is present. I have taken this vow before, but today I take it finally and keep it finally. He can talk. In fact, nothing can stop him talking; but I won't.

There is a possibility that Artie may come home on leave today. I sure hope he does. On Friday we got a letter through from Cuthie. It was written July Seventh, practically four months ago. He said he was well, and that he had talked with some other fellows from the R.A.F. and from what they told him he realized he was very lucky to have escaped unharmed as he did.

Last week I began to scribble again.

EPISODE #22

- TUESDAY, NOVEMBER 5, 1940 -

Guy Fawkes Day

It is U.S. Election Day. In the eight o'clock news this morning I was very amused to hear that last night Wendell Willkie held the air, giving his last campaign speech, for an hour and a quarter, "assisted by Bing Crosby and Mary Pickford." This is simply ridiculous. It is as though Churchill should broadcast to the Empire assisted by Jack Payne and Cecily Courtridge.

Last night was a very bad night again, the Germans making up for all they didn't give us on Sunday night. Fourteen bombs have been dropped in this immediate vicinity. South Street is a mess. It is shut from the public from Victoria Road to the Market Place. There are big craters in front of the Havana and in The Plaza Car Park. Also in front of Boots and the police station. There are unexploded bombs in Ives Nursery Gardens, in Errol Road (Bertie's Road), in Gilbert Road, and one nearly opposite this house, between here and the main road.

We have had notice to keep all our windows wide open. There was another bomb in Eastern Road, and I don't know where the rest are, but there are fourteen in there, three or four blocks. I don't know how many in the rest of the town. We are now, four fifteen p.m., having our seventh warning for today. What shall we get tonight? Ted has decided to move the bookcase out of this dining room, and bring in its place the parlor sofa. This is a good idea. For two months he has been sleeping on the floor, in front of the bookcase, but if a blast tumbled the bookcase on top of him, the books would almost surely kill him. Anyhow, it's getting too cold to sleep on the floor. So we have this shifting job to do this evening. I have been carrying lots of the books into the parlor, but now must rest, as I am too tired to do any more. Artie didn't come home last night, so I'm afraid we shan't see him this week after all.

- *WEDNESDAY, NOVEMBER 6, 1941* -

Roosevelt is in. Good.

Forty-three bombs were dropped on Romford on Monday night. One lodged in the Gasometer. Captain Davis has been here today to remove it. This is the engineer who successful removed the bomb from St. Paul's. News from Rome: Last Wednesday the Pope blessed two hundred Italian officers, received in audience, saying to them, "We bless all you who serve the beloved fatherland with fealty and love." So they were off to invade and destroy Greece, with the Pope's blessing. My God! What decent English person could remain a Roman Catholic!

- *THURSDAY, NOVEMBER 7, 1940* -

When my new young charwoman arrived this morning, she had seen last night's destruction on her way here. She passes the water-works, and she tells me four more houses are completely demolished there, and others, more than she could count, on Clydesdale Road and Melrose Avenue. She was very shaken, and very angry. "They didn't tell you these things," she exclaimed. "It is only when you see for yourselves that you know." That's right. Specific news is never given out; on the BBC everything is minimized. We, the public, only know what happens in our own localities, and that we are never officially told about. We have to suffer or to see for ourselves, and then we know. On, this devilish war! When will it end?

It is a busy day. Mrs. Jude here to lunch, and Rita Pullan to tea.

- MONDAY, NOVEMBER 11, 1940 -

Armistice Day

I went out this morning, my first outing since the end of June. I walked all around the block, down this road to South Street, along South Street to the Market Place where I went into Adam's to buy some articles, then up the Market to Stone's, then up further to Junction Road, and then down Junction and home. It is one square block. I am as tired as though I had climbed a mountain. Into the doctor's this afternoon and she said I shouldn't have walked so far.

"Down to the end of the street and back would have been ample," she said. I expect so, but I wanted to do some shopping. Commodities are becoming scarce. The shops seem only to have what they have on hand; as their supplies give out they apparently are not able to obtain renewals. Prices are soaring too. I chiefly wanted some scales and a new coffee pot, some Pyrex ware, and some knives and scissors. I also wanted a milk saucepan and a double boiler, but these I couldn't get. Anyhow, in all I spent three ten; this is a lot of money to put into hardware.

Mrs. Thomson was here to tea.

- *TUESDAY, NOVEMBER 12, 1940* -

It is a very stormy day. News of further earthquake shocks in Romania. The oil fields are reported destroyed. Good! This will save our R.A.F. the job.

Good air report today also. Yesterday we were raided all day long. In all we had eight alarms, though the last all clear came through at nine fifty p.m. We had a raidless and quiet night, thanks to the storm, which was terrific. Yesterday the enemy came over in groups of one hundred and fifty. With them was one lot of Italian bombers, eighteen in all. Of these, our boys brought down thirteen, in the Thames Estuary, and the others turned back without showing fight. So that's another smack for the dirty dagoes. The Greeks are punishing them too; of an Italian Battalion of twelve thousand men, in the mountains to the north of Greece, the Greeks have destroyed about two thirds, and the rest have run away back into Albania, leaving most of their equipment, guns, field kitchens, even personal belongings, behind them, strewn through all the ravines. The Italians don't want to fight. In the Mediterranean they won't bring their navy out. Then why don't they overthrow Mussolini?

Today Molotov has arrived in Berlin, bringing a suite of sixty-five specialists with him. What for? Russia also doesn't want to fight. She only wants to stand by and pick the bones.

Ten a.m. The first raid of the day is in progress. Wednesday night was fairly quiet because the weather was very stormy, but last night, though misty, there was moonlight and we had a very bad night indeed. Barrage was very heavy; we heard bombs falling, but whereabouts in this neighborhood I have not heard. BBC reports the raids last night were worst "in a midland town where the casualties reported are very heavy." But it was pretty bad in Romford too. Yesterday Ted told me that Tommy Skilton had been hit again on Wednesday night, this making the third time he has had it, in addition to having his workshop on North Street destroyed. Wednesday night was the worst for him. The bomb took the roof completely off his house, and fell through into his kitchen, blew out everything and blew to bits even his bicycle, which was in his shed. Mrs. Skilton is terrified, and wanted to leave at once. Naturally!

Three twenty p.m. I was interrupted by the incursion of my neighbor, Mrs. Thomson. I seem doomed always to have some female leech around. I have had peace from this woman for three weeks, whilst she was in Devon, but she came home on Tuesday this week and seems to think she has to come in to see me every day. She was here all Thursday afternoon and now all this morning. She's a darned nuisance.

Ted would be rude to inconvenient visitors and markedly show them the cold shoulder, but I can't be rude to people, hence I get stuck with all the bores in town. The raids are continuing all day. There was much gunfire at dinnertime, and what sounded to be hundreds of planes flying over, but we could not see them. The one o'clock news told us that the worst raids last night were on Coventry, on the scale of the first heavy raids on London, and that there are at least a thousand people killed, and much of the city destroyed. Glorious war!

When I opened this book to note this morning, it was with astonishment at the depth and tenacity of our aversions. Yesterday whilst we were at dinner there came a very important sounding knocking at the door. When I opened it I saw two nuns, one of whom accosted me by name, saying, "Mrs. Thompson! You remember us? We used to call on you at your other house, don't you remember? The Poor Clare's of Woodford?"

Immediately anger rushed through me. "Wait a minute," I said, but closed the door in their faces. Had the door been un-shuttered, so that I could have seen through the glass panel, I should not have opened the door to them, for I will never willingly open my door to any nun.

I came in to Ted, and said, "There are two nuns here, begging. You had better see them. Don't bring them in here." So he left his dinner at once, opened the door to them, and invited them into the parlor. They conversed together for a while, and then he showed them out again. When he returned to his meal he actually had tact enough to say nothing.

Was I angry! They were looking for a meal, of course. Where did they pry out our change of address? And come here to beg? I did not recognize the one who spoke to me, but she knew me all right. I had a shock when I opened the door to them. I could think of nothing. Anger and hatred suffused me on the instant. God! How I loathe nuns! So deep is this hatred in me that I was physically upset for hours. My heart increased its beat, and my legs and hands were trembling until after I had my tea. This is what Ted's lunatic religion can do to me.

I have been busy cooking today. Artie does expect to get leave this next Monday so I made a batch of pastries this morning, and since dinner I have mixed up a couple of fruit cakes, which are now in the oven. Presently I am going to make flapjacks, and tomorrow I'll make a chocolate layer cake and some fudge. If I can stock the pantry with homemade goodies before he arrives, we'll have more time for talking when he does get here.

- *MONDAY, NOVEMBER 25, 1940* -

Artie didn't come. His leave was cancelled, but he was promised leave on the twenty-fifth, so perhaps he'll come today. I don't know where last week went. I did get some letters written but nothing else.

Yesterday Ted invited young Mr. Simpson in to tea. When Simpson was received into the church this year, Ted was his godfather. Now Mrs. Simpson and the baby have evacuated to Ireland, and Simpson is waiting to be called up. Meanwhile he is boarding at Haga's. All the talk yesterday was of the absurdities and idiosyncrasies of Haga. Haga is the town quack; and he is another religious manic. He is an excessive Protestant; brought up in Norway as a Lutheran, he is a heretic from Lutheranism. He was a stanch First Day Adventist once, but he left that faith also. Instead of becoming an indifferentist or an agnostic, he still remains actively religious, but he can find no sect to agree with, and has a religion apparently all his own. Of course, he is violently anti-Catholic.

Psychologically, Haga is explainable. Now, nearly sixty years old, he began his life as the son of a poor Norwegian farmer, a pious Lutheran. He had very little education, but was thoroughly indoctrinated with a fervent Lutheranism. At about the age of twenty he left Norway, and he has never returned there. He went to India, and also to the States, making his living as a masseur. Somewhere on his travels he married a Welsh girl, another ignorant person.

In 1903 he came to England, picked out Romford on the map, and settled here. He continued to make his living at massaging. Now he added hydropath, sunbathing, Swedish exercises, light treatment, etc. He set himself up in a house, and began advertising his cures. Perhaps he did make cures. Anyhow, he succeeded in making a living, and bringing up a family. He writes to the paper practically every week in the year, instructing the public either on his special field of medicine (so called) or on his special brand of religion. So far as this goes he is one of the town's jokes.

You see, nobody takes him seriously, and he is a man without any real anchorage in life. By profession he is definitely a quack; the real doctors in town will have nothing whatsoever to do with him. By religion and by nature he is a wanderer; he has left his native land and his native religion. He has no country, no religion, and no profession, and he has married a foreigner, so his very children are half and half's, so nothing about him is genuine; everything is half-fake. His evangelizing is the way to compensate his ego.

Last night Simpson was full of tales about how Haga behaves in his own house. He is definitely an eccentric, we laughed about him. It was unkind, but he is laughable. What I noticed was the unconscious assumption of superiority on Ted and Simpson's part simply because they were Catholics. This is laughable too, but they don't know it.

Haga is a muddle-head, but neither Ted nor Simpson thinks for himself. They accept the authority of the church. Why? Because they feel they need an outside authority. Haga is authority for himself. It just depends what kind of person you are.

Simpson is another weak specimen of a convert. He has swallowed all the bait. He is an ordinary fellow, respectable, but ignorant, educated sufficiently to make a living, of course, but without culture. Ordinary. I can't stand the ordinary. He is one of the respectable lower classes. I can't stand the lower classes! They may be saints, but oh they bore me! I detest this mania for theology that men get. Whether it is, Ted or Haga or Simpson, they're all the same. Why theology? Isn't it because theology doesn't require either brains or learning? They can read it up in books and memorize it. It's easy. Real knowledge, science, or mathematics, or philosophy, or engineering, or music, or doctoring, need a keen and alert intelligence, practice, and a trained mind. In short, a genuine ability and a good education. If a man is a dud in a real science the fact is immediately apparent, but if he is a fool for even a wise man spouting theology, nobody can prove him either right or wrong, and neither the error nor the correctness of his theological opinions will make any difference to his practical life.

As I see it, theology is the cheap diversion and solace of the half-educated and the half-baked. I've never known a strong man bother himself with theology. So, Simpson, another of Ted's duds! To lack a proper education, a classical education, what a lack! These poor fools talk about God and Heaven and Hell and think they have knowledge, and oh, I'm so weary of fools!

EPISODE #23

- TUESDAY, DECEMBER 10, 1940 -

Artie came on the twenty-fifth and left again the following Monday, a week ago. We had a quiet time, on the whole, whilst he was here, though we received a bad bombing on Friday, November twenty-ninth. Then things were fairly quiet again, with no alert at all throughout Saturday night last, the seventh of December. Sunday also was a quiet day, but last Sunday night we had the worst bombing that has happened in this town yet. South Street, North Street, London Road, Old Church Road, the Market Place, very much damage done. Also the Telephone Exchange demolished, operations buried in the debris, awful! Our old section near Westwood practically completely demolished. The number of casualties is not yet known.

Then yesterday was quiet, and a quiet night again last night, quiet so far today, but what will happen tonight?

It is four p.m. and Miss Coppen has just been in. She only came back from Devon a week ago and arrived home in time for Sunday's slaughter. Happily there was no serious damage in her locality this time. She had only to endure the noise, and the fear, of course.

This morning I was writing letters to America. The censor returned a long letter I wrote to Jim and Doris,

November eighteenth, to me a few days later, also parts of a letter I wrote to Harold. It seems no information about times and places of air raids must be mentioned to anyone abroad; it might help the enemy! This is sheer nonsense. The enemy knows what he has done, anyhow. Further how can he possibly get hold of the mails? Further what good would it do him to know the names of the obscure suburban streets on which his bombs fall? Especially when the news is weeks old? Oh, the silly censorship!

- *FRIDAY THE 13TH, DECEMBER, 1940* -

Foggy, but we have been out. Ted bought himself a new overcoat this week, so I ventured to ask if I could buy some new underwear. After some talk, of course! Ted said I might buy some. I quoted a figure of from three pounds to four pounds, but actually the bill comes to four/nineteen/six. When he gets it, he'll expostulate, but the garments are bought, and not before I needed them. The last time I bought winter underwear was in New York, in 1933, and I have patched and patched these 'til they are now only fit for floor clothes. Of course I had hopes of renewing them again in New York. But when shall I get to New York again? These English garments are clumsier and less well cut and well-tailored than the American ones, but they are wool, and expensive. Still, they are the best I can get in England.

Saw the town. The devastation is tremendous, but everywhere workman are clearing up, boarding up the broken windows and renewing shop fronts with planks and beaverboard. There isn't a piece of glass left from Latham's Corner to the Romeo at Raynham Road. Exchange Place, where the biggest bomb fell, is one indescribable heap of rubbish, which looks as though it could never be cleared up.

One curious thing I noticed in the town, and that was a sense of exhilaration. The streets were as crowded as usual, but people looked more alive than usual, sort of excited. There was no gloom. Everybody seemed to be smiling, ready to chatter and laugh. It's as though the town knows it has suffered the worst, and now it says, let them all come! We don't care a damn!

- SUNDAY, DECEMBER 15, 1940 -

Ted is playing for High Mass. I just want to say, I'm happy. No reason, just happy. Perhaps it is a general feeling everywhere that the tide of fortune has changed, at last we are beginning to win the war. There has been a terrific defeat of the Italians in Egypt this week. This morning's report says we have taken over thirty thousand Italian prisoners in Egypt, with all the tanks, guns, equipment, and supplies. The Greeks too continue to beat the Italians in Albania. It's heroic. Then, besides, Petain has forced Laval to resign from the French cabinet, and this morning's report is that Laval has been placed under arrest. At least this means that French public opinion is changing. Maybe the French are recovering from their defeatism.

The day is cold and frosty. We had a good sleep last night. No warnings yet since that all clear which sounded at eight-thirty p.m. last night. Ted slept upstairs in bed, but I remained down here in the dining room. I don't think I shall ever be able to stay upstairs 'til the war is over. Had a good sleep just the same. When Ted went out to church, had a good bath by the fire, and dressed in my new Jaeger combs. Also put on two new plasters.

Altogether I'm feeling very comfortable and very fit. Now I am going to cook the dinner. Actually have a piece of beef today, two pounds fourteen ounces of rump. This is marvelous. Beginning tomorrow the meat ration is to be reached again. Anyhow, here's roast beef for today. Oh the roast beef of Old England, and Oh the Old English roast beef! That's a song that was always mixed up with the Christmas carols when I was a child. So long!

- *MONDAY, DECEMBER 16, 1940* -

The first, the greatest, and the most everlasting factor for the intelligent married woman's happiness is financial independence. I've said this before and I'll say it again, and I'll repeat it on occasion until I die. Love is a chimera, religion is a broken reed, but money in hand is an unbreakable blessing, and without it life progress is all over snags. Have just had words with Ted over luncheon about Stone's bill. It is for five pounds. After a harangue and a scolding, he refused to take it with him. I had asked him please to write me a check for it, but he said, "I'll take this up with you again."

Of course, this will give him a second occasion to nag me again. I notice that whenever Ted has to pay out money for my personal expenses, he is always most reluctant to do so, and very disagreeable about it. He has bought himself underwear this winter, eight shirts, four pairs of shoes, a raincoat, and an over-coat, also handkerchiefs. I have bought no clothing at all, until now, when I have bought only underwear. To buy this I first had to ask permission! When he asked what it would cost, I replied, I didn't know perhaps about three or four pounds. He hemmed and hawed about it, but finally said all right, I could get myself some underwear. I did not know what it would cost. I have never bought myself underwear in England. So, my estimate was too low. I went one pound over it. That's my usual fault. I am so afraid to ask him for money, I always put the figure as low as I can, and practically always I say something too low. It's always like that.

Ted seems to think a wife should cost nothing. Deep in his old sub-conscious must lay the Victorian conviction that a wife and mother must give all, endure all, and receive nothing. He was sarcastic about Dr. Keighley's bill. I've no right to be ill, it seems. Every time he has to pay out real money for me he hates it. I ought to cost nothing, and I never ought to want anything. Oh dear, he is a trying man! I didn't handle him right. I ought to have bought new clothes twice a year every year of our married life as a matter of course. I never did. I made my clothes last, until now he seems to have the notion they ought to last forever. The dress I am wearing now is made over from a dress I bought new in 1933 to go to America in! Then it was shop worn, and offered at the bargain price of a guinea! I ought to throw my clothes away every season, the same as other women do, but alas, I haven't the habit.

Yes, to have money of my own, what heaven that would be! I still keep the dammed household accounts book. Every penny I spend has to be written down, and once a month it is all analyzed into a big book Ted keeps. It is so silly. His passion for figures makes household and personal accounts a burden. Oh, for money of my own, for a life of my own, for freedom! I want to have money without asking for it, to spend it without accounting for it. Why shouldn't I? No. Not with Ted for a husband.

- TUESDAY, DECEMBER 17, 1940 -

Ted, at breakfast: "Who eats the brown bread I occasionally see on the table?"

"I get it for possible visitors, and sometimes I eat a piece of it myself."

"All right, so long as it is eaten. Don't buy it for me. I don't eat it you know. Don't buy so much bread."

I buy one small whole-wheat loaf once a week, on Saturdays. Ted has to interfere in trifles. What has the housekeeping got to do with him? This is a good example of his petty carping. Oh, he is an exasperating fellow!

At dinnertime I had to ask him to bring me one pound tonight, for tomorrow's laundry, etc. I was scared to death to ask him, but had to. Then he surprised me by saying, "and where's your Stone's bill? Give it to me now and I'll write you a check." So I've actually got the check without being compelled to ask a second time for it. Of course he presented with it another harangue on spending, and I said naught, though privately I thought him very silly.

- FRIDAY, DECEMBER 20, 1940 -

A bad raid this morning, which frightened me considerably anyhow. I am in a very depressed frame of mind. Ted is on my nerves most frightfully. He talks and he talks, such drivel, and I'm so bored. My constant judgment on Ted is that he's a silly fool. He talks such rubbish, about the war, and about religion, or, rather, about Catholicism. He's so fanatical and so puerile, oh my God; I do get so weary of him.

I am weary. Do you know what? I want to be happy. I am so tired of everlasting seriousness of life with Ted. I don't want conferences about trifles. I want to be careless.

I hate the everlasting debating and arguing, all of it mostly about nothing. I'm always being called to account. I hate it. I'm so tired of housekeeping and of meal getting. I gave Ted a dish of spaghetti, tomato cheese for his lunch today. He complained it was too wet; all the water in it held the heat. I said I was sorry, but he went on for half an hour about my extraordinary ideas about cooking, and what he calls my knife, fork, and spoon dishes. So silly! That's Ted for you; he can't ever stop talking. He says the same things over and over again. He is as repetitious as Selma, and as Bert. It's a family characteristic, I suppose. What weariness to those who have to listen to them!

Yes, I'm tired, tired of the house, tired of the husband, tired of myself, and damnably tired of the war. I want ease and love and laughter. I'm tired of the glooms, sick to death of war.

- MONDAY, DECEMBER 23, 1940 -

I've many letters to write and don't want to write one of them. The older I grow, the less and less I like writing letters, in fact, I detest writing them.

We had a bad night again last night, but I notice I am not as frightened as I used to be, which shows one can get used to anything. I also notice I don't pray anymore. Why? Is it because I am convinced God doesn't care, so why bother Him? Or is it because I am so fed up with Ted's religiosity that I am drained of all religion? Or because I am so disgusted with all the religious piffle, which is so interlude in the BBC programs, I feel I cannot add an iota of my own to what I have to receive from the air?

Anyhow, I'm not praying. It is not that I am feeling particularly irreligious. It simply is that I don't feel to need religion nowadays. Ted, if anything, is more religious than ever. When he will talk about it, I am bored to extinction. His fanaticism becomes even more extreme. When he came back from Mass yesterday, I was listening to a religious service on the radio. The BBC broadcasts at nine twenty-five on Sunday mornings a religious service, conducted on Anglican lines, but with the address given by prominent laymen. Yesterday's address was by Henry Brooke, M.P. Ted always makes sarcastic comments on these items. Yet, when an R.C. Service or sermon is broadcast, he always listens attentively. The fact is that Ted cannot allow validity, authenticity, or even sincerity, and positively not knowledge, to any religious sect except the Roman Catholic. His bigotry is extreme. Literally for him there is only one true religion, the Roman Catholic religion.

Deliberately I say Roman Catholic religion for it is a religion all of its own. Ted never speaks of Christianity. He only speaks of Catholicism, by which he means Roman Catholicism, and no other. He really believes all the other Christian sects and churches are in error, a vast concourse of heretics. When I was listening to the Anglican prayers and collects yesterday, I thought how dignified and how lovely they are; and, like a fool, I said so; to which Ted immediately countered, that they were only translations from the missal. I didn't say anymore. They are not all translations from the missal; many of them are originals to the English Prayer Book, but what would have been the good of saying so? Ted will not allow goodness or beauty to any prayer or devotion outside Rome. Oh, what weariness his pettiness is!

When he came back from benediction in the afternoon, I thought again what an essentially selfish religion Roman Catholicism is. The Catholic is only concerned with his own soul, saving his own soul. He does not go out to help the afflicted; he does not attempt to better the world. He does not speak of God, nor of Christ and the teachings of Christ, he only speaks of the church, and the teachings of the Popes. The Catholic is only concerned to keep himself in a state of grace, so that he may avoid Hell, primarily, and get to Heaven eventually; about his neighbor, for good or ill, he is not concerned at all. It is "God and myself," as Newman has said. Yes, myself. In the world, there is something very callous about the Catholic. He is so sure he is one of the elite, and he doesn't give a damn for any other fellow. Talk about the masons being cliquey; they're not in it with the Catholics!

One day last week I met Father Bishop in Ives Gardens. We chatted about the war for a few minutes. What else is there to talk about? As I noticed him in the street I couldn't help thinking how unimposing he was. To begin with he has an insignificant appearance; a short man in clerical clothes, a raincoat too big for him, a soiled white neck cloth, an enormous hat, going green with age, and a cheap cardboard attaché case. This shabby and soiled appearance is inexcusable. Father Bishop has plenty of money, private means. Besides, as Wesley wrote to one of his Chaplains, a pastor should dress well and keep his clothes neat and clean or he is a very poor advertisement for his God.

I also noticed Father Bishop, in the cold, showing a purple-tinged nose. I didn't exactly have a sense of revulsion from him, but I thought to myself, how can I ever have thought that this man could ever have advised or helped me in any way at all? What does he know? Whatever use is he in the world? What is it to being a priest, to say mass, to administer the sacraments, to pray? What is that in this world today? Father Bishop doesn't even teach school; he doesn't do anything at all that is work. He is "busy" with his church, yes, but what a lot of play acting that is! After all, it is only inside his church that he has any importance at all. In his cope, he is impressive, but that is the impersonal impressiveness of the archaic actor. In his rectory, wearing Cossack and biretta, he has a dignity of office; but on the street, my, he has no dignity at all. On the street he doesn't even seem to be a man, only just some sort of a neutral block of flesh perambulating. Yet I like Father Bishop. As a man, as a director, I hold him of no account at all.

Ted was talking last night about what the world might be after the war, and saying that the Pope ought to be asked to the conference table for the peace. Ted thinks the Pope the most important man in the world. The world doesn't think so. After all, our ancestors fought bloody wars to throw the Pope out of politics, so I hardly think statesmen will take him by the hand and invite him back into politics today. Besides, he is an Italian. I don't think any Italian will ever be asked for his advice in the administration of democracies.

Well, I must write my letters, so Au-Revoir.

EPISODE #24

- FRIDAY, DECEMBER 27, 1940 -

We have lived through one of the strangest Christmas's I have ever known, yet I was happy, happier than I have been at any Christmas since we left America. Ted and I were quite alone.

There was actually a lull in the war. We had no raids Tuesday, nor Christmas Day, nor yesterday, which was Boxing Day; nor during the nights either. The war began again this morning. Gerry was overhead during dinnertime, and the one o'clock news reported a heavy dueling this morning with the long-range guns across the channel.

Midnight Masses, the first mass for Christmas Day, were celebrated during the afternoon of Christmas Eve, because of the blackout, a special dispensation from the Pope being given for this. The real midnight mass, from the Benedictine Abbey of Downside, was broadcast by the BBC. This was weird. Here we lay, in this little room, rolled up for the night on our sofas, and in the darkness we listened to the mass, sung by the monks. We also kept our ears pricked listening for an alert to sound, because we didn't know Hitler wasn't coming. It was beautiful. As always, the *Adeste Fideles* brought me to tears, and also to prayer. I was melted and able to pray. I prayed especially for Cuthie.

Ted rose early and went out to the eight thirty mass. I did not go of course. I don't think I can sit out any service, or any movie show, either, until the war is over. After breakfast we had callers. Mary Bernadette Jude and Rita Pullan. Edna Renacre came up for Christmas Eve. For dinner we had chicken and a plum pudding; for supper, veal and ham pie and a plum tart. Ted went to bed early. He went upstairs and wanted me to go too. It was too early, only nine thirty, and besides, I cannot even try to sleep upstairs. Again, we didn't know Gerry wasn't coming.

So, I stayed down here by myself, and enjoyed myself quite thoroughly. First of all, there was music from America. Then a play by Edgar Wallace, *The Squeaker*, and then Henry Hall and his band until midnight. Some of the tunes were so compelling, I even got up and danced by myself two sides round the table, all the room I had. It was good. I felt happy. Then there were some new songs, very funny, which made me laugh right out. The absurdist was entitled, "Never swipe your sweetie with a shovel." Really very funny, or so I thought on Christmas night. Then I listened to the midnight news, and then I put out the light and settled myself for sleep.

Ted rose early and went to the early mass, then, whilst we were still breakfasting, Lily, my newest charwoman, arrived to do her Thursday work. No visitors, but a lovely day.

On Christmas Day, after I had finished clearing up after dinner, I thought I'd dress for the day, so I took out my red velvet dress. I found it much too big for me. I wore it just the same, but I was pleased! I shan't wear it again as it is entirely too large all over, and has dropped so much that the hem lies on the floor. I think I shall take off the velvet skirt and lower sleeves, and lay the lace and silk top away to be utilized for some other evening gown some other time. The velvet I will match, if I can, with some woolen stuff, then make the whole up into an afternoon gown, using the velvet to make a draped surplice bodice, and the wool for a skirt. As soon as the sales come on, if there are going to be any this January, I'll go shopping for dress goods. Anyhow, I feel like new clothes. I want to be happy, I want to feel nice, and to look nice, and I feel like sewing. I feel I can't let the war get me down anymore. I'm going to smarten up in every possible direction. I won't be sad. I won't be fretful. I'm fifty-six, but I'm going to be as happy and as beautiful as I can possibly make myself for the next thirty years. The war has got to end sometime. Meantime, I'm still alive, and intend to do my utmost to stay alive.

Ted slept downstairs last night. We had a real pleasant happy evening together. Ted can be charming when he wants to be. Lights out as the clock struck eleven, but we both overslept this morning. Ted did not wake until eight thirty-five a.m. I had been awake some time, but had been lying waiting to hear the clock strike eight. You may be sure that I wasn't going to start the day by waking Ted. We could lay abed until eight o'clock every morning if only he could give up going to early mass. However, he was very good-natured, and we had a happy breakfast together. Then off he went to the office. So the holiday's all over, and here we are, on joy-trot again.

- SATURDAY, DECEMBER 28, 1940 -

Eleven thirty-five a.m. Ted has just gone out to pay the bills, change the library books, go to the barbers, and to confession, etc. We have been having a cozy morning with the papers beside the fire, myself having intermittent trips to the kitchenette to pay the tradesman, see the garbage man, fix a stew, and so on.

The German night raids began again last night. There was a very big attack on London. The barrage was terrific. It began promptly at eight o'clock, and went on without ceasing until eleven p.m. Then it died down, and the all-clear came about midnight. It was bad here in Romford too. Bombs kept on falling. One terrific one seemed to fall right in our back garden. However, it didn't. I don't know yet where they did fall, though at church this morning Ted heard there was a landmine fallen in Gidea Park again. Perhaps that was the most awful one we heard. As usual, attack seemed to be concentrated further over toward the station, so I suppose poor old Victoria Road got it again. What a life.

I had most pleasant dreams. I was dreaming of when I was a girl, working in St. Martin-le-grand, and Ted was the handsome foreign stranger, knocking at the door. It is seldom I dream of my girlhood days. Last night every detail was clear and correct. I even dreamed of the very clothes I used to wear and had forgotten 'til sleep brought them back to my mind. I was having a lovely time, and so happy, and excited too, like I used to be in girlhood. Perhaps my resolutions against encroaching old age brought my youth back to my dreams. Or perhaps it was a sort of delayed action dream, contingent on Ted having received a Christmas letter from Fred Phillip, in which he told us of the retirement of Tiddler Raison. Anyhow, I was back in my girlhood in St. Martins-le grand, and life was being a thrilling adventure. Good! I hope I can dream of my girlhood some more. My dreams have forgotten I was a mother, almost as my waking hours have forgotten the fact. I was just merely myself, my young self.

Have been reading Andrea Maurois's book, *The Art of Living*. I liked it. Here is one idea he quotes from Goethe. It seems Goethe once wrote: "It is absolutely necessary to break people of the habit of dropping in on you unannounced. They insist on you concerning yourself with their affairs, and their visits fill your mind with ideas foreign to your own. I myself do not need such ideas; I have more than I can do to carry my own to their proper conclusion."

How heartily I agree with Goethe about this. For these past two weeks I have been free of the visits from the lady next door. Her husband is at home on the sick list. As soon as he goes back to work, I know she'll be on my doorstep. I intend to protect myself from her troublesome time-wasting visitations. I've got my writing to do, and I intend to do it too. I feel in fine form, and I'm going to write steadily, every opportunity I can make.

Milkman has just been. He tells me the worst damage last night was in Balgores Lane, which is completely wrecked. They also got the gun crew at Marks Gate. At the top of Carlton Road is an unexploded landmine, all the people evacuated. Another mine happily fell in the tennis courts. Barking and Barkingside got the very worst of last night's packets.

- SUNDAY, DECEMBER 29, 1940 -

Am sitting with my back to the fire, drying my hair. I haven't washed my hair for myself for years, but today I felt I just had to. It is about six weeks since I was at the hairdresser's, but it has been feeling so greasy and so itchy this past week. I'd got today to the point where I couldn't wait another day to go to the beauty parlor. So as soon as I had finished washing up the dinner dishes, I fixed a shampoo and have given my head a fine wash. I also cleaned all the households' combs and brushes. Of course I can't 'set' my hair. A professional will have to do that. Also, I am debating with myself whether to have my hair cut short again or not. For nearly a year now I've been pinning it in a bun on my neck, but I'm getting tired of the bun; tired of the hairpins and the hard knob of hair, which is in the way of my hats. Of course, if I have it off, I expect I shall immediately regret it, yet I am tired of it as it is. Having long hair cut off is very like other mistakes of a woman's lifetime; like leaving your country, or changing your church, you never can go back properly to your originals.

Ted is at church, and I'm hoping he won't invite Simpson back to tea. I am not exactly dressed for visitors; in a towel and my hair hanging down to dry. We had a most awful explosion at exactly noon today, and a blinding flash of light accompanied it. Ted was in the parlor and did not see the flash; but I was in the kitchen, standing at the sink, and I thought the very sun itself had fallen into the room, and I wasn't even facing the window. I was awfully frightened, and shook for an hour afterwards. There was no alert on, so we presume this must have been a delayed action bomb exploding somewhere nearby. There were no raids hereabout last night.

Last night I was dreaming of Cuthie. He was dressed in a blue lounge suit, but with decorations on his shoulder. We were out walking together, and he was holding my elbow, as is his custom. I was also dreaming of my girlhood again, and back even further than before. I saw myself sitting on St. James Park Station, waiting for a train. It was a Sunday morning, very still and quiet, and I was the only person waiting for the first after church train to come, like it used to be, often, when I was returning from Swallow Street. A vivid dream of the girl I was, and remaining with me all day, but the girl is a stranger.

Memories. I have thousands and thousands of them. How am I ever going to pin them all down in a book? I feel I must hurry. When death strikes now any hour, any day, any night, I want to express all that I know, all this that I am, and all that I was, before death can strike me. I want this for my children. When in the future some of them say, "I wonder what sort of woman Mother was, anyhow!" I want them to be able to look into the mirror of a book, and find me. So I must write quickly and steadily. From day to day, I will write what I can, and if I cannot write consecutively, then those who find my writings must sort them into their proper order and so make the sequence correct for themselves.

- MONDAY, DECEMBER 30, 1940 -

At six o'clock last night the raids began again. The all clear did not sound until just before midnight.

Nothing fell here in Romford, though the zooming was incessant. This morning, however, we are told the main attack was on London, the heart of the city, and that hundreds and hundreds and hundreds of incendiary bombs were literally rained down. Among the buildings damaged were the Guildhall, another Wren church, two hospitals, a museum, and several schools. Except for naming the Guildhall, no names were given, but the report says it was a wholesale attempt to destroy London completely by fire. Eighty horses were killed when a high explosive fell on a brewery. Several shelters were hit, and railway stations; no properly military objectives were attacked, and the enemy appeared to be concentrating on setting fire to as many buildings as possible. When is all this deviltry going to end? The rest of the world for the remainder of time, I think, will hate Germans.

I'm restless today. For one thing, the day itself is dismal. I rung up Lillian Young's early this morning, to see about getting my hair set, but her assistant answered me, telling me Lillian was away for a few days because her husband was home on leave, though probably she would be back at work tomorrow. However, I did not make an appointment. In these times, when nobody can tell what may happen tomorrow, I think it's useless to make any sort of an appointment ahead of time. So, with my free empty morning, I wrote some letters and made out some new library lists. I could not write any of my own stuff because I could not settle to thinking.

Bad luck that free time should coincide with a bad mood! However, I rung up Lambert's and have ordered some books. First of all, Mrs. Vivian Hugh's latest, *A London Family Between Two Wars*. I need to follow Mrs. Hughes work. Next, a book reviewed in last week's *Times* Literary Supplement, *An Anatomy of Inspiration*, by a Dr. Rosamund Harding, and lastly, *Ideal Weight*, by W.F. Christie, described as a practical book for outpatients. It costs less than a visit to Dr. Keighley. Anyhow, I've ordered it. Then I read in Proust. So far I find him even more enjoyable on a second reading than on a first, but I do think one needs to be a Catholic and to know France to extract the very utmost pleasure from him.

President Roosevelt made a great speech last night. Ted actually woke me up at three thirty this morning to tell me Roosevelt was on the air! We tried to get through, but could only get music. I was sorry. I would have liked very much to hear the real voice, making the real speech. However, we were given many excerpts from it in the one o'clock news; good, but not so good as hearing it in the first historic moment. He was calling to the Americans to give all aid to Britain. Harold, back in the summer, thought America would be in the war by January.

Now I'm going to get a cup of tea. I'm most horribly restless. I hope I am not suffering a premonition of something.

It was a quiet night, due, most likely, to bad weather.

This afternoon I went to the hairdressers and had my hair properly set. I did not have it cut. Now it looks nice again. Will try to get to the hairdressers regularly every fortnight during 1941.

Further reports on Sunday night's raids on London. It was evidently an attempt to destroy the entire city by fire. Uncountable thousands of incendiary bombs were dropped, and practically old historic London was burnt down. The Guildhall is gone, Trinity House and eight Wren churches. What vandalism!

Commenting on this vast devastation to Ted this evening, I inadvertently let myself in for a long evening's monologue; in particular the loss of Wren's Churches gave him a fine springboard for his criticizing. He said the churches weren't beautiful, weren't used, and Protestantism was dead anyhow. Then he enlarged his discourse to condemn modern art and modern religion, about which he knows nothing of either. He kept on nearly the whole evening, and I sat grinning like a Cheshire cat, I suppose. Oh, I was so bored. I kept on noticing Ted's mouth. When he monologues, he scarcely opens his lips, or his teeth either. He speaks very quietly in a monotone, and his mouth is one thin straight line. It was a horrible and cruel mouth.

I have Jacob Epstein's, *Let There Be Sculpture,* to read.

AFTERWARD: THOUGHTS ABOUT RUBY'S DIARY & GENETICS

Written by Adele Aldridge on her grandmother,
Ruby Alice Side Thompson

I began keeping a diary when I was twelve years old. My experience is that while private diaries and journals may tell truths that are not revealed 'out loud' they do not tell the whole truth. When the writer of a private journal dies, even if those journals are made public, as Ruby's are here, they can't possibly tell the parts of the life that are lived and not written about, nor how others viewed the writer.

I mention this issue because in reading through my grandmother Ruby's very private writings, she has repeated complaints about how her husband treated her. I have become thoroughly annoyed with my grandfather Ted. I had heard that he was a devout Catholic but had no idea that he was also a very narrow-minded arrogant bigot. And while I am sure that Ruby was telling the truth about how she experienced Ted, I know from my own journal keeping that the truth in the writing is not the whole story. I believe that Ruby used her diary as a safety valve for her emotions. She writes numerous times when she is exasperated with Ted to the point of wanting to scream. She tells us that she does not confront Ted with her feelings about his infuriating behavior.

Ruby's ongoing dissatisfaction with her marriage and the obvious emotional starvation that she experienced was a situation that young people today would not understand, given that half of the marriages today end in divorce. Ruby was well aware that Ted's fanatic Catholicism would make a divorce from Ted impossible. Added to that fact, in those days women were considered property and treated as such. I am sure that Ruby was not alone among women of her generation who had to endure a marriage that they felt trapped in.

Given Ruby's continual anger and disappointment with her husband, I am amused by the fact that as angry as Ruby gets with Ted, year after year, he is able to win her over in bed, which she refers to simply as "loving." She doesn't write about their "loving" times in specifics, but she refers to these encounters as assuaging and apparently satisfying. I have to conclude that as impossible as Ted was with his continual petty criticisms, the two experienced "chemistry." The miracle and mystery of physical chemistry between two people is that it can override all other factors in a relationship.

I get the picture from reading Ruby's diaries that there was no one in her life with whom she could share what was really on her mind. In many instances, I found Ruby to be ahead of her time in her thinking. The feminists of the 1970s would have loved her. And, of course, her views about Catholicism, the Pope, nuns, the Irish, men, and the war in general, are bound to upset some people. This was a private diary and now that anyone mentioned in it are all dead, I think Ruby's views deserve to be published just as she wrote them.

I believe that people today have no concept of what it was like to live through those bombings during the war. Thank God! Imagine living in New York City and the surrounding suburbs not knowing, when you went to bed at night, which buildings would be still standing, how many people would be killed; not for just one night, but too many for me to comprehend as a living reality to endure.

I have been wondering about genetics and how our DNA might relate to my habit of keeping a diary. No one directed me to do so. I doubt that anyone in my family even knew about my diary. So I can't attribute my own diary writing, which continues to this day, to anything in my environment. I wrote because I enjoyed the physical and mental process. Where did that desire come from?

When I was a child, no one thought I looked like my grandmother Ruby, who was very stout, so it was a shock to everyone in the family when a picture of Ruby at the age of twenty was sent to us from England. Ruby didn't look much like her older, heavier self in this picture. She looked like me. When my daughter Vicki saw these pictures side by side, her response was, *"You look like her clone."* I have to wonder if my own diary-keeping obsession is as connected to my DNA as is having a strong resemblance to Ruby.

One day, after beginning this project, I did a little meditation on the subject, asking myself, asking Ruby, *"Why should I take my precious time to do this beyond the fact that I believe the subject matter is worth publishing now? I have a pile of unfinished projects of my own to complete. Why yours?"* The answer I came up with in this meditation was that my negative reasons all had to do with ego. I remembered that one quarter of my DNA comes from Ruby Alice Side Thompson. It sounds corny but one quarter of Ruby lives in me and she wants completion. So be it.

My interest in diaries and journals goes beyond my own and my grandmother's personal recording of events. Among other adventures in journal writing, I published an edited version of approximately seven years of my journals in my PhD thesis at The Union Institute & University in 1981. My core faculty was José Argüelles. This degree, a first of its kind in the study of, "Art and the Personal Symbolic Process," contained content from my journals including dreams, daily life, active imagination, drawings, and my work with the *I Ching*.

I took my journal on a different journey.

- THE END -

This volume was compiled by

VICKI WASHUK

Victoria Aldridge Washuk is the Great Granddaughter of Ruby Alice Side Thompson. Vicki received a B.A. in Psychology from Fairfield University, and currently lives in Milford, CT. She is married and the mother of three daughters.

London Blitz Diary Blog
http://womanlondonblitz.blogspot.com/

BIG WORLD
NETWORK
.COM

www.ingramcontent.com/pod-product-compliance
Lightning Source LLC
Chambersburg PA
CBHW060918040426
42445CB00011B/689

* 9 7 8 0 6 1 5 8 5 8 9 4 4 *